A Deluxe Edition with 14 New Homebrew Recipes

EXTREME BREWING

An Introduction to Brewing Craft Beer at Home

Sam Calagione
owner of Dogfish Head Craft Brewery

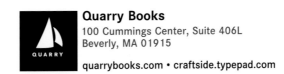

Quarry Books
100 Cummings Center, Suite 406L
Beverly, MA 01915

quarrybooks.com • craftside.typepad.com

First published in the United States of America in 2012 by
Quarry Books, a member of
Quayside Publishing Group
100 Cummings Center
Suite 406-L
Beverly, Massachusetts 01915-6101
Telephone: (978) 282-9590
Fax: (978) 283-2742
www.quarrybooks.com

Library of Congress Cataloging-in-Publication Data
Calagione, Sam, 1969–
    Extreme brewing : an enthusiast's guide to brewing craft beer at home / Sam Calagione.
        p.   cm.
    Includes index.
    ISBN 1-59253-293-4 (pbk.)
    1. Brewing—Amateurs' manuals. I. Title.

TP570.C3146 2006
641.8'73—dc22   2006019246
                                                                                     CIP

ISBN: 978-1-59253-802-7
Digital edition published in 2012
eISBN: 978-1-61059-948-1

10 9 8 7 6 5 4 3 2 1

DESIGN: Lori Wendin

PAGE LAYOUT: Leslie Haimes

COVER DESIGN: Rockport Publishers

PHOTOGRAPHY: Kevin Fleming, except the following:
    Courtesy of Yakima Chief, Inc., 12; 13; JohnSchulz/www.studiodschulz.com, 67

Printed in China

THIS BOOK IS DEDICATED to all of the amazing brewers I am and have been fortunate to work with at Dogfish Head. Your dedication and passion for the craft of brewing inspires me every day.

Contents

Foreword
to deluxe edition

A COUPLE OF YEARS AGO I was fortunate enough to be invited, by Sony and the family of Miles Davis, to brew a special beer commemorating the fortieth anniversary of his fusion masterpiece album, *Bitches Brew*. In reverence of that fusion approach, we created a beer that fused three-parts imperial stout fermented with raw dark sugar from the Ilse of Mearitious with one-part Tej—the traditional honey beer of Ethiopia, which is bittered with gesho tree root.

I met Miles's nephew, and onetime bandmate, in a recording studio in New York to tell him about our plan for the recipe and to hear some early outtakes from the *Bitches Brew* recording sessions. I told him what we planned to make and about the list of ingredients we would use in the recipe. He was quiet for a minute, as we nodded along to the music. Then, he said, "I like the sound of that ... it reminds me of something Miles used to say: 'Don't play what's there, play what's not there.'"

THERE HAS NEVER BEEN A MORE EXCITING TIME TO BE A BEER LOVER

Homebrewers and craft-beer lovers are promiscuous, and this is a beautiful thing. They are explorers, and they love the thrill of something new. They might have a cadre of go-to breweries or recipes on which they focus most of their attention, but they are also ready and willing to step outside their comfort zones and let their freak flags fly. Being adventurous is what makes the wide world of beer so thrilling. There has never been a more exciting time to be a beer lover. There are now more than 1,800 commercial breweries in the United States alone; this number recently surpassed the pre-Prohibition high, and the average American now lives within 10 miles (16 km) of a local brewery. As consumers, we finally have a huge variety of commercially brewed, diverse, and flavorful craft beers at our fingertips. And yet the homebrewing movement has never been more vibrant and innovative. At first glance this might seem counterintuitive. There are more styles of more brands of high-quality world class craft beer available in stores and on tap at restaurants than ever before, and yet people are gravitating to homebrewing in droves.

In the 1970s, when the modern homebrewing movement began gaining momentum, a driving factor was the lack of diversity and the lack of intensely flavorful American beers available in that era. It was part of the DIY approach—if you can't buy something, make it yourself. Fast-forward to today: Store shelves are bursting with choices, craft brewery marketshare is at a record high, but homebrewing continues to grow as well. I believe the reason for this growth goes back to this ideal of promiscuity—the joy that comes with pushing the envelope and stepping outside of your comfort zone. As a homebrewer, you are not limited by what beers are available to buy; you are limited by what ingredients are available to buy, and if you consider the entire culinary landscape as your playing field, you are then truly only limited by your imagination.

WHAT'S THE DEFINITION OF EXTREME BREWING?

There's a passage in Colman Andrews's fine biography, *Ferran*, about the eponymous chef who is rightfully recognized as the patriarch of the molecular gastronomy movement, which I believe also defines the raison d'etre of the extreme brewing movement: "On one occasion Ferran rather cryptically remarked, 'Why do we have coffee and then an egg at breakfast, while at lunch we eat the egg and then have the coffee? If you understand that, you can do avant-garde cooking.' What he meant—I think—was that if it occurs to you to notice such contradictions in the way we eat, you'll be more likely to question the common culinary wisdom and then be able to imagine ways to countermand it. Ferran wants us to eat with our brains."

Extreme brewing, to me, means using your own brain and not someone else's idea of brewing tradition to make extremely flavorful beer. Not just the four common ingredients pounded down our throats by the largest global brewers with the force of billion-dollar ad campaigns. It's about refusing to accept the idea that beer can only be made with barley, hops, water, and yeast. Flipping accepted practices on their head, deciding for ourselves as brewers what the widest definition of beer can be, and helping to more broadly define beer by exploring the outer edges—there's avant-garde art. There's avant-garde cooking. Why shouldn't there by avant-garde brewing?

Tristan Tzara, one of the papas of Dada and the avant-garde art movement, wrote in his manifesto, "The new painter creates a world, the elements of which are also its implements, a sober definitive work without argument. The new artist protests: He no longer paints a reproduction of what he sees but creates directly in stone, wood, iron, tin, boulders—locomotive organisms capable of being turned in all directions by the limpid wind of momentary sensation."

In addition to wood, stone, and iron, avant-garde brewers are adding grains, herbs, spices, fruit, and other wonderful elements to this list of inspiring "locomotive organisms." There are dozens of creative recipes in this book, and I wish you luck and big fun reproducing them at home. But I mostly hope that reproducing the tried-and-true recipes of the avant-garde brewers who contributed to this book gives you the confidence to, in time, take a jazz solo of your own; step outside the sheet music of these recipes, and add your own distinct music—a pinch here and a teaspoon there.

As beer drinkers, all of our palates are unique, so the qualities we are looking for in great beers are also unique. This is why there are so many different beers out there. It's subjective. The definition of extreme brewing is subjective as well. I asked a few friends for their definitions, and you can see that they put their own spin on it. But we agree quite a bit on what makes extreme brewing, extreme.

Short's Brewery, in Michigan, makes many envelope-pushing beers like Idia Sprice Pilsner and Bloody Beer. Here's what my buddy Smokin' Joe Short, of Short's Brewing, has to say: "In my opinion, extreme brewing draws people to the 'what ifs' of possibilities in fermentation and science. Kind of like what the gold rush of the 1840's did for the miners or what thoughts of settling in the New World brought for the early pioneers. It's all about the excitement, the unknown, and the potential rewards of forging possibilities for that next awesome thing. As a species of evolution, I think we're drawn to new experiences and we continue to seek things that make us happy and mystified. That's what extreme brewing does for me. I want to discover what is possible and enjoy the feeling of accomplishment that comes with successful experiments, and I think consumers do as well. I think we've only just begun to realize the potential beer has. As with food, there are infinite possibilities, and as beer is food, I can only imagine what is to come."

And here's what my friends Jason and Todd Altrom, who run BeerAdvocate, the largest online beer community in the world, had to say: "Extreme Beer: [noun] A beer that pushes the boundaries of brewing."

That's it. A style, alcohol-content, and ingredient-free definition that is flexible; as creative brewing should be.

Extreme Beer Fest is BeerAdvocate's signature event, which since day one has been dedicated to celebrating brewers who push the boundaries of brewing by raising a fist at the norm. And that's definitely a major draw for consumers. The market is flooded with sameness, so when something creative comes along, people are compelled to try it. And of course, the small-batch rarity of many extreme beers generates even more of a demand to try them.

Dogfish Head has been the proud sponsor of BeerAdvcoate's Extreme Beer Fest for many years, and the growth of this festival certainly correlates with the growth in excitement around the extreme brewing movement. This year the 2,200 EBF tickets sold out in two hours!

You can see a common theme emerge as we work to collectively define extreme brewing—uncommon beers. It's about pushing the creative boundaries. When I opened Dogfish Head almost two decades ago, we were brewing 12-gallon (45.4 L) batches at a time on glorified homebrewing equipment. We were nano before nano was cool. Now we make more than 6,000 cases of beer each production day. But every week we are brewing with exotic ingredients such as saffron, organic brown sugar, raisins, and orange flesh. As brewers, we are more experimental than ever, and we still approach what we do with the curiosity and passion of homebrewers.

This week at Dogfish Head, I'm wood-pressing organic fuji apples for a cider-beer hybrid brew we will do at the pub. This recipe also features fresh cilantro and dried cayenne peppers. I worked up the recipe with a musician friend of mine who is also an adventurous foodie. I'm also working with a molecular archeologist and an Italian craft brewer to resurrect an ancient Etruscan beer that was brewed with tree resins and pomegranates. There is as much value and creative potential in looking backward for creative brewing inspiration as there is in looking forward.

—Sam Calagione

Foreword

by Ken Wells

I FIRST STUMBLED UPON Sam Calagione's name a little more than three years ago when I began to do nascent research for the book that would become *Travels with Barley: A Journey through Beer Culture in America.* At that point, all I knew was that I had a publisher willing to send me cross-country to drink beer on an expense account and write about it. I wasn't a beer geek; I was an enthusiastic amateur about to set out on the pilgrimage of a lifetime. My job was to illuminate beer culture in America and fill in the 300 or so pages expected of me in some clever fashion. A guy wouldn't want to blow such a great assignment, and I was suddenly desperate to hook up with clever brewers who could help me plot my route down America's river of beer.

I hadn't yet encountered the term "extreme beer," but as soon as I heard of Sam and his brewing philosophy, he didn't strike me as your everyday brewer. I'd learned of the Midas Touch project, in which Sam had teamed up with a biochemical-archaeologist from the University of Pennsylvania Museum to re-create a beer whose recipe had been reverse-engineered from dregs found in drinking vessels at the bottom of a 2,700-year-old royal tomb in Turkey. (Some think the gold-laden tomb forms the basis of the King Midas legend, hence the beer was named in homage of the monarch who turned everything he touched to gold.) It started as a one-off project, the beer to be served at a celebration of the mythical king's birthday, but Sam crafted the brew with such verve that it soon became a commercial success.

MY FIRST THOUGHT was that brewers who painstakingly re-created these historical beers might form a chapter in my book. But after talking to Sam on the phone, I got an inkling that making beers from recipes gleaned from the tombs of dead kings was but a subset of a far more interesting phenomenon. Sam, being the gregarious soul that he is, immediately invited me down to his Dogfish Head Craft Brewery to talk about Midas Touch and other projects he was brewing up.

Sam was a lucky call, as he turned out to be one of the cannier and more inventive practitioners of extreme beer, a commitment by the gonzo element of the craft brew crowd to take beer where it's never been before. (Well, OK, those monks in Belgium have taken beer to some pretty curious places over the ages, but bear with me.) The relevant point is that extreme beer is equal parts theater and cutting-edge brewing, but it's also about bringing energy, excitement, and edge back to one of man's oldest organized endeavors. Meanwhile, for the experimentally minded beer consumer (and I am now avidly one of those) it has brought a raft of deliriously interesting and tasty beers to the market. And for the experimentally inclined homebrewer, well, extreme beer is the mountain you must climb. And this book's for you.

A short time after our first meeting, Sam took me on a tour of the Dogfish Head skunk works. He had in his brew tanks at the time an experimental batch that he knew I, as a recent self-declared hopshead, would be intrigued by: a seriously huge India Pale Ale (IPA) with an International Bittering

Unit (IBU) rating way off the charts and an alcohol by volume (ABV) level of about 19 percent—and the beer wasn't yet done fermenting! He called it 120-Minute IPA because, though brewers traditionally add their hops at the beginning and end of the boil, Sam had come up with a process by which he continuously hopped the beer for a 120 minutes using a proprietary robotic-pneumatic gizmo he'd invented called Sir Hops Alot. The first robo-hopper, in fact, was one of those goofy, circa-1978 electrified vibrating football games, canted at an angle and rigged up with a 5-gallon bucket of pelletized hops over the boil kettle. The contraption kept shorting out, so Sam had to design a Sir Hops Alot as a more permanent fix. Of course, it turned out there was good brewing intuition to this madness: the continuous hopping infuses the beer with delicious hoppy flavors while tempering its bitterness.

We sampled the 120 Minute right out of the tanks and I realized this was not a beer to to sip while watching a baseball game. (Drink more than one, and you'll be asleep by the fourth inning.) But it was a wildly interesting IPA (and, in fact, the strongest of its style in the world) and it would make for great small talk in my next assemblage of beer geeks. (Heck, even the Bud Light minions I interviewed for my book would declare "are you serious?" when I'd tell them about 120 Minute being finally bottled at 18 percent ABV, more than four times stronger than their, uh, under-achieving favorite beer.) I recall pressing Sam to explain to me how he and other like-minded brewers were achieving these astonishing alcohol levels in beer when for centuries, brewers had found it impossible, outside of distilling it, to get brews much up above 15 percent ABV. Sam coyly demurred, saying only that he'd used several pitches of proprietary yeast strains. And though he wouldn't say what the strains were, he quipped: "If you looked at the yeast under a microscope, you'd see lots of leather skirts, whips, and chains." Somehow, I've never been able to think of beer yeast in the same way after that quote.

SAM, OF COURSE, wasn't quite done experimenting with hops on the extreme beer frontier. I later caught up with him at the Blind Tiger, a well-known Manhattan craft brew bar, where he debuted what appeared to me to be the world's first commercial … hops bong—a contraption stuffed with fresh leaf hops that took hopping to another level by infusing hops between the tap and the pint glass.

Sam, being Sam, had his own name for this device: an Organoleptic Hops Transducer, aka Randall the Enamel Animal. To date, about 300 Randalls have been pressed into service around the country in the name of sublime hoppiness. I didn't think Sam could one-up Randall that night but he actually did, taking the stage with his two-person hip-hop (or would that be hop-hip?) group the Pain Relievaz and, powered by some Randall-infused 90 Minute, started rapping about beer. (If you're ever around Sam, you have to get him to do "I Got Busy with an A-B Salesgirl.")

Now, as for this book, *Extreme Brewing: An Enthusiast's Guide to Brewing Craft Beer at Home*, there's nothing particularly dangerous about it if you use it according to Sam's instructions. Just don't try to drink what you make in one night. My sense is that this is as much a book for beginning brewers as it is for those who've already brewed a few (or many) batches and would like to move on from making the same old amber ales. Sam's not joking about the title. In this book are recipes (and step-by-step brewing instructions) for beers with names like Dark Star Licorice Stout, and Blood Orange Hefeweizen. As a bonus, Sam also throws in some recipes for beers from his brewery including his 60-Minute IPA (which in my humble personal opinion is one of, if not the, best-balanced IPAs on the planet). Oh, and by the way, Sam (a man with far too many talents) also turns out to be an extremely able writer and the book is filled with helpful helpings of beer history, lore, and inside dope on the extreme beer movement.

So open it up, kick back, and brew yourself some Dark Star Licorice Stout. (And invite me over if it turns out well!)

Ken Wells is a longtime writer and editor for the Wall Street Journal *whose page-one piece on extreme beer in April 2003 was the first mention of the movement in the popular press. He's also written three well-received novels of the Cajun bayous and edited two anthologies of* Wall Street Journal *stories. He's currently finishing up his fourth novel and also writing a book about Hurricane Katrina in his home state of Louisiana.*

Introduction

THEY SAY YOU NEVER FORGET your first time. I know that's certainly true for me. The first time I brewed a batch of beer was in 1993 on the stovetop in a friend's apartment in New York City. I had recently discovered some of the great beers that were being made by upstart American craft breweries, beers made with passion and creativity that were a complete departure from the watered-down, mass-marketed styles so popular at the time. I had also been introduced to some bold-flavored imports that, with their rich, centuries-old heritages, were infused with flavor and character. Although I was intrigued with these styles, it wasn't until I actually made a beer for myself that I fully understood, appreciated, and ultimately became obsessed with, the art of brewing.

THE ART OF BREWING

Most people don't consider beer making an art form in this day of multinational brewing conglomerates and automated brewing equipment. But the brewer's art is alive and evolving in the small, independent breweries and homebrew enclaves that are thriving around the world. True, the brewer's art is ephemeral; it is an art that is consumed, but so is the art of musicians, actors, and dancers. When done well, when done memorably, the effects of each of these art forms can stay with the person who experiences them for a long, long time. Possibly, even, forever.

Every time you pick up a newspaper or watch the news you hear about branding. It's a term that has escaped from the boardrooms and invaded our culture. Supermarkets are branding their own products, clothing companies are extending their brands into the world of home furnishing, and global brewers are diversifying their brands with endless line extensions and acquisitions. It seems as if every business entity out there is focused on building a brand with a unique, highly marketable image. The result, of course, is that we're all suffering from brand fatigue. But when you make and enjoy a batch of homebrew, it's like hitting the pause button on an overwhelmingly brand-saturated world to reconnect with the most important brand in your world: you. Something built sturdily and lovingly from your own hands and mind has no need for the reassurance of status or the validation of market share. It's special

because it comes from you. And the beers that you make will be a modest, unconventional, but very real reflection of who you are. In this hectic day and age, what better gift could there be than to share a handmade batch of craft brew with friends?

Though the beer you brew is an obvious end, the process of making it is not just an end but also a means unto itself. As you make the different beers outlined in this book and gain the confidence to eventually create your own recipes, you will be participating in the brewing tradition, a tradition that is as old as civilization itself. You'll soon recognize your own latent talent for making something special with your hands. You'll get to know the smell and feel of the individual ingredients. You'll come to love the sound of your beer bubbling away as it ferments and the way your kitchen smells like a bakery as you boil the barley juice and add the hops. In their own way, these nuances will come

to matter as much as the way your final beer tastes, because you are *making* something. Brewing is a nature-based hobby that restores a measure of humanity and perspective to the art of living.

GOING TO EXTREMES

While there isn't a single quality that is the alpha-aspect of a great brewer's profile, there are a number of qualities that all great extreme brewers share, to a degree. By extreme brewers I mean those making beers that are not made in the image of the dominant style of the day (i.e., light, homogenous lagers). Extreme beers, as will be discussed in this book, are beers made with extreme amounts of traditional ingredients or beers made extremely well with nontraditional ingredients. The people who make these kinds of beers, both professionally and at home, share a curiosity for how things work, and a passion for breaking free from the crowd (in this

case boring, watery beer), a desire to put their own thumbprint on the world, and a propensity for risk. But, good homebrewers are also disciplined. They understand that they must first have a strong grasp of the traditional brewing process before heading off on their own tangent to subvert and influence that tradition. If you recognize these qualities in yourself then you are well on your way to becoming an accomplished homebrewer.

BREAKING AWAY FROM THE NORM

From the day I opened Dogfish Head Craft Brewery in 1995 our motto has been "Off-centered ales for off-centered people." This perspective influences everything we do and everything we make at our company; it implies that we do not brew beers that maintain the status quo. We never will. While we have focused on making strong exotic brews since our inception, in no way would

we want to pretend that Dogfish Head invented extreme brewing. The tradition began well before Dogfish Head was around. Sierra Nevada, Hair of the Dog, and Anchor Brewing are but some of the earlier American practitioners of extreme brewing though the method certainly didn't originate here. I don't think any beer enthusiast would argue with me when I say that extreme brewing is rooted in the brewing traditions of Belgium—a country surrounded by some of the most storied grape-growing regions of the world that capitalized on the assets of its own climate and indigenous crops to brew the most interesting, food-friendly beers the world has seen. This book will celebrate the Belgian extreme brewing tradition and explore the ways in which Belgian ingredients and methods can be incorporated into various recipes.

Some of our first recipes at Dogfish Head were for beers made with maple syrup, roasted chicory, organic Mexican coffee, juniper berries, apricots, pumpkins, and brown sugar. Our beers were noth-

ing like the ones found in cans and thirty-packs on the shelves of liquor stores in the mid-nineties. We had some challenging years before the beer community grew and became as self-educated and exploratory as it is today. There weren't many takers for the thirteen-dollar six-packs of oak-aged, maple syrup-fermented beers we were selling in 1996. But we never discounted the value of our hard work and quality ingredients by dropping our prices. Like a homebrewer, we brew first for ourselves and second for our friends, loved ones, and hardcore beer enthusiasts. Thankfully, the community of friends and beer enthusiasts has continued to expand as our company has grown up. Today, Dogfish Head is one of the fastest growing breweries in the country. I'm proud of that but I'm even prouder of the fact that we have achieved this heady growth while always focusing on making the kinds of beers that are honest reflections of our own idiosyncratic, envelope-pushing selves, not the me-too beers that the world already has too many examples of. That being said, more and more people are discovering the full-flavored diverse beers being made today by American craft breweries, import breweries, and

homebrewers. It's comforting to see so many brewers helping to stretch the boundaries of the definition of good beer along side us.

As you make and share your first batch of homebrew, remember that this book is only one of many guides that will lead you on your journey. There are a number of other great homebrew books, websites, and magazines that are referenced in the Resources section. As you become more comfortable with the steps involved in the brewing process, intuition will become your guide as you explore the art of extreme brewing. Don't get discouraged if every batch doesn't turn out perfect. As long as you follow the proper steps, most batches will turn out perfectly drinkable and in time, you will go from making good to great beer. You'll also discover that no two batches will taste exactly alike. No two snowflakes are exactly alike either, but in their own beautiful way each is perfect. What will remain constant is your ability to reflect your own passion and tastes in the beers that you make. Congratulations on your decision to join the ranks of the world's most extreme brewers.

PART 1

Getting Started

WHETHER OR NOT you have attempted to homebrew before, it's important to grasp the basics of brewing ingredients and processes before moving ahead, attempting recipes from this book, or elsewhere. As things become clearer, your comfort level with the practical aspects of brewing will increase. And as you gain confidence, you'll be more capable of embracing less traditional methods and ingredients. In short, before you can successfully take beer in a new direction, you need to understand exactly what goes into it and become familiar with the tools that are necessary to make it.

CHAPTER 1

Ingredients

THERE IS A SEEMINGLY limitless selection of commercially available beers on the market today, from light lagers to dark stouts and from tart wheat beers to roasty porters. But why not make your own? Basically, anyone who can cook a good soup can make a halfway decent beer. Like any art form, brewing affords you, the "cook," the opportunity for some artistic self-expression. The art of brewing begins with the selection of ingredients. Just as a painter uses different oils, watercolors, and charcoals, the ingredients that go into brewing allow you to express your vision of the perfect pint.

To the uninitiated, it may seem that brewing is a complicated scientific process. In a way it is; the conversion of starches and carbohydrates to sugars, and the subsequent conversion of sugars to alcohol, are chemical processes. However, just because there is some basic science going on while the brewing protocols are being followed, doesn't mean that making beer needs to be a complicated endeavor. This chapter will demystify both the ingredients and the process.

THE BIG FOUR

Barley, hops, water, and yeast are the primary constituents of a brew. Barley, a cereal grain rich in starch, is a prime source of sugar and gives the beer "body" due to its gluten and protein content. Hops, a type of plant grown worldwide and used primarily for beer making, adds flavor and bitterness to counterbalance the sweetness of malt, while also acting as a preservative. Together, barley and hops add "color" to the final product. Yeast contributes some flavor and aroma to beer, but its primary function is as a catalyst for the fermentation process. Yeast eats the sugar from the barley (or any additional sugar source) and converts that sugar into alcohol. It's as simple as that.

Whether you choose to order your ingredients from a catalog, an online retailer, or your local home-brew store, quality is the number one priority when seeking out ingredients.

Barley

Barley is grown all over the world. Brewing barley begins as a seed within a husk. Both unmalted barley and malted barley appear the same in their grain forms. Malted barley is soft enough to be cracked between your teeth. Unmalted barley is very hard, and the starches within are not readily accessible.

The process of malting barley and wheat is fairly complicated and best left to the pros—you needn't convert your spare bedroom into a floor-malting facility in order to make good beer. To malt barley, a maltster (someone who works at a barley malt facility) creates a warm and wet artificial growing environment so that the seeds will think they have been planted in the soil. The barley is first piled up in mounds and then sprayed with water until germination commences. When the grains begin to sprout, the pile is then spread out to encourage the germination process; during this time the hard inside

Adding yeast to the carboy is the catalyst for fermentation.

of the seed, called the endosperm, changes into a softer carbohydrate substance (starch). Germination is permitted to proceed to the point where the maximum amount of accessable starch exists within the husks. Once this point has been reached, the sprouted grains are shifted into a kiln to dry, which halts the germination process and toasts the barley. The grain has now been malted. If the grain is kilned or dried at lower temperatures, it will be relatively light in shade and contribute less color to your beer. Darker malts, like those used to make stouts, porters and bocks, are kilned at higher temperatures.

Commercial breweries use vessels called mash tuns to combine hot water with varieties of milled malted barley (and sometimes wheat) in different volumes for different recipes. First, the milled malted barley and warm water are mixed in the mash tun. This mixture is brought to a stable temperature at which enzymes convert the starches in the barley into sugars that will then be available for fermentation. The bottom of the mash tun is perforated like a giant colander. After the grain and water steep like tea for an hour or so, liquid drains out the bottom of the mash tun and is pumped over to the

This malt was made from partially germinated, then roasted barley.

A cool ship at a commercial brewery in Belgium receives wort from the boil kettle the old-fashioned way. The cooling wort is exposed to wild yeast and bacteria that is in the air, which facilitates fermentation.

boil kettle. The grains in the tun are sparged (rinsed) with more warm water to ensure that all of their residual sugars make it into the boil kettle as well. This prefermented beer, known as wort, is then brought to a boil. When you make your own versions of the recipes in this book, you will use prepared malt extract that will allow you to skip the steps of malting, mashing, and sparging.

Malt Extract and All-Grain Brewing

Most recipes in this book use small volumes of specialty and dark grains in the same way that a commercial brewer would, but the bulk of the barley source will come from the extract base. The malt extract that will be the main source of fermentable sugars in your brew was prepared in a malting facility. The process of making malt extract involves brewing wort and removing water by means of boiling and withdrawing moisture by way of a vacuum. Unfortunately, this intense condensing process robs the syrup of natural compounds in the barley that are conducive to thorough fermentation. Loose translation: The yeast cells that will ultimately eat and ferment the barley sugars prefer all-grain wort over all-extract wort. So while the potential difference in quality between an all-grain beer and a partial-grain beer is not all that significant, the potential difference between an all-grain beer and an all-extract beer can be much more noticeable. All-grain beers generally taste better, but well-made extract beers can be equal in quality.

The biggest difference between the two methods is evident when making a very light colored beer. The malt extract process tends to darken the sugars some when compared to the yield of a partial-grain batch. As previously mentioned, the older the malt is, the darker it will appear. The malt kits sold at homebrew shops and in catalogs generally have a two-year shelf life. By using some amount of specialty grains in a bag, you are replacing some of the natural compounds that will be absent from your malt extract. A measurement scale called Lovibond often identifies the colors of malts and barleys (e.g., 20 Lovibond). The lower the Lovibond number, the lighter the color.

Hops

Without hops, all beers would be cloyingly
sweet. Hop vines grow well in many different
regions of the world, but only produce healthy
cones within certain latitudes. In its natural
state, a hop flower looks like a miniature, soft,
green pinecone. If you rub a few fresh hop
flowers between your hands you'll notice that
your palms will immediately get tacky. Inside
the hop cones are the sticky resins and oils
that are most abundant at harvest time. After
harvest, the hop cones are laid out and dried
until the majority of moisture has been wicked
from the flowers in order to allow them to age
without spoiling. There is a fine line between
drying the hops too much, (which robs them
of their flavor and aroma enhancing properties)
and not drying them enough (which will cause
them to go bad). Once the hops are properly
dried they are either vacuum-packed whole or
condensed into pellets and vacuum-packed to
await their journey to home and commercial
breweries.

Hops can be grown in almost all zones and
regions of the world. In the United States,
the growing conditions in Washington are
ideal for hops. When conditions are right,
homebrewers can procure a hop rhizome and
grow hops at home.

The most common vessel in which brewers use their hops is the brew pot (at home)
or the boil kettle (at a commercial brewery).
The earlier that the hops that are added in the boil, the more they
will contribute bitterness to the taste of the beer. The later in the
boil that hops are added, the more they will contribute to the aroma
of the beer. Many brewers play around with adding hops postboil
on the way to the fermenting tank or carboy (a large, usually glass,
juglike container generally used to ferment and age beer) or even in
the fermenting tank and carboy. This is called dry hopping. Once
the boil is over and the wort has settled, it is ready to be chilled and
transferred to a fermentation tank or carboy. The temperature at
which it should ferment depends on the type of beer that is being

made from the wort. If a lager yeast is going to be used the beer will be transferred at around 45°F (7.2°C) for fermentation. If an ale yeast is going to be used, it will be transferred at about 70°F (21°C) for fermentation.

Water

In terms of proportion and volume, water is the main ingredient in beer, yet the importance of it is rarely touched upon in brewing recipes. When you add hops to your beer, you know you are adding only hops and it's relatively easy to estimate the effect that the volume and type of hops being added will have. Water is a little murkier, so to speak. Almost all natural water supplies (municipal, spring, etc) will have different levels of ions, minerals, gases, and even potential pollutants. Municipal water supplies may even have residual levels of chlorine that retard the fermentation process. However, odds are that if your municipal water supply is fine for drinking, it's fine for homebrewing.

Before Hops

BEER HAS been brewed with hops only since the thirteenth century. Before that, brewers in different parts of the world used a broad range of herbs and spices that were indigenous to their homeland in order to counter-balance the sweetness of the barley.

> *Because homebrewers often try to make their beers in smaller pots, they have less-than-ideal headspace to allow for a vigorous boil. A bigger brew pot helps. A vigorous boil means better hop utilization and better breakdown of all of the added sugars.*

The ideal profile of water is pretty broadly defined; you are basically looking for soft, bacteria-free water that will work well for brewing, cleaning, and sanitizing. As is the case with commercial brewing, you will use a lot more water in the homebrewing process for cleaning and rinsing than for the actual brewing. Most municipal water sources provide clean water that will generally be adequate for homebrewing.

There are a several ways to find out more about your water. If you pay a water bill to the town, give the water resource authorities a call. They are required to supply you with an accurate analysis of the water they provide. If you obtain your water from a well, then you will have to pay to get it analyzed by a water quality laboratory. The local government (county, township, extension office, etc.) usually has some listings for private water testing. Check the phone book for one of these or look up a water-treatment equipment company. If they sell the equipment, they are usually prepared to test your water for free. You can also discuss the water quality with other homebrewers and homebrew supply store workers who have probably already considered the effects of a given water source's profile on different styles of beer.

There are two basic choices with your water supply, provided it is potable and odorless. You either use it the way it is, or you change it to meet your brewing needs. Your choice will likely depend on how technically involved you want to get with your brewing. Some homebrewers do a little of each—they mostly use the water they have and add a tablespoon of gypsum (a mineral consisting of hydrous calcium sulfate) or a pack of water salts (calcium compounds also known as brewing salts) to replicate certain traditional brewing styles.

HISTORICAL NOTE

Drunk as a Monkey

This expression comes from witnesses of monkeys behaving erratically after eating piles of fruit that had fermented with wild airborne yeast. The only extra step that man has added to the natural process is boiling the barley sugar water to remove wild yeast and bacteria to prevent the final product from possible spoilage. Basically, the brewing process is as simple as combining natural ingredients and nudging a natural process in the direction you want it to go (toward your pint glass!).

Dry Hopping

Vinnie Cilurzo,
Russian River Brewing Company

THERE ARE SIX important components to dry hopping: quantity, time, temperature, mixing, multiple dry hop additions, and yeast contact.

1. Quantity At Russian River, on average we dry hop at a rate of 1 pound (455 g) to 2 pounds (907 g) per barrel (31 gallons [117 L]) of beer. This is the equivalent of ¼ ounce (7 g) to 1 ounce (28 g) of dry hops per gallon of homebrew. The amount of dry hops you add to the primary or secondary fermenter depends on how aromatic you want your beer to be. There is no formula to figure out ahead of time to determine what the end aroma will be in your finished beer; this is strictly trial and error. I can give you some broad guidelines but this is really something that is subjective—a big enough aroma for you may not be enough for me. It is my opinion that aroma is one of the most important components of an IPA or a Double IPA. On average, I go with ½ ounce (15 g) per gallon (3.8 L). When we use an ounce (28 g) per gallon (3.8 L), it is made via multiple dry hop additions over a four-week period. In most cases, we use pelletized hops rather than whole-leaf hops to dry hop with. If you are a beginning brewer you'll definitely want to use pellets. However, as you progress and gain more confidence you can begin to experiment with hop cones. Using pelletized hops gives you a quicker

release of hop oils, whereas dry hopping with hop cones gives you a slower release of their oils and a more subtle hop aroma.

2. Time The second point to consider is time. Again, there is no formula for this, and only continued experimentation will yield you useful knowledge for future brews. I like to dry hop our standard Russian River IPA for seven days, our Blind Pig IPA for ten days, our two Double IPAs (Pliny the Elder and HopFather) for twelve to fourteen days, and our Triple IPA (Pliny the Younger) for four weeks. Regardless of how long you dry hop, one of the most important things you can do for making a quality beer is to keep a carbon dioxide blanket on top of your beer in the primary or secondary fermenter. If you are an advanced homebrewer, you may have a CO_2 tank from your draft keg system. But, if you are a beginning brewer, all you need to do to keep the fermentation lock floating gently and rock the fermenter for a few seconds. This will release some CO_2 out of the beer and into the headspace of your fermenter. This is especially important if you are dry hopping your beer in a plastic bucket, as they don't seal as well as glass carboys. If the inside plastic piece of the fermentation lock isn't floating, there probably isn't a good CO_2 blanket in the fermenter. Also, remember that since your homebrew will be sitting for an extended period of time, it's important to keep the light out. If you're aging the beer in a glass carboy, cover it with a large, black plastic trash bag. Light and hops don't mix; when beer comes in contact with light, even for just a few minutes, it creates a skunky flavor. In order to keep an eye on the CO_2 blanket on the beer, try cutting a small hole in the top of the trash bag for the fermentation lock to fit through.

3. Temperature For most homebrewers, temperature is not a problem since the beer will be sitting at room temperature. In my opinion, dry hopping between 52°F and 72°F (11°C and 22°C) is critical to getting a big hop aroma in your beer. If the beer is any colder, you won't get as much hop oil extracted into your brew.

4. Mixing The idea of mixing, or rousing, the dry hops back into the beer during aging is new even to many professional brewers. At Russian River, to drive the dry hops back up into the beer, we push carbon dioxide through the bottom of the tank. This effectively puts the hops back in suspension. For homebrewing, you can actually accomplish this simply by rocking the fermenter gently. This will get the hops back to floating in the beer, thus giving them more contact time. I like to do this five days before the beer will be transferred off the dry hops.

5. Multiple Dry Hop Additions Another idea that is new to many professional brewers, and is most certainly considered extreme, is multiple dry hop additions. In most cases, I add a second dry hopping at the same time that we push the initial dry hops

back into the beer, five days before the beer is transferred off the dry hops. The one exception is our Triple IPA (Pliny the Younger), which gets four separate dry hops additions. Two weeks after primary fermentation, I add the first dry hop addition. After the initial dry hop, I continue to add the next two dry hop additions in one-week intervals. The final dry hop addition takes place in the serving tank at our brewpub. If you are bottling your homebrew, just give it one more week in the fermenter with the fourth addition. I'd suggest 1/2 ounce (15 g) per addition; sometimes less is more when dry hopping.

6. Yeast Contact The sixth and final decision you will need to make when dry hopping is whether to transfer your beer to a secondary fermenter after primary fermentation. This will get your homebrew off the yeast. I find that the more yeast I can remove from the beer before I add the dry hops, the more hop aroma my finished beer will have. With more yeast removed, the hops will have more surface area in contact with the beer to extract more hop oil. These oils will give your beer a big, rich hop aroma.

After more than twenty years of brewing both at home and professionally, I still continue to experiment when it comes to dry hopping. It is one of the most elusive aspects of brewing, but also one of the most enjoyable parts.

Another adjustment that can be made to improve the water would be to remove any residual chlorine. This is a fairly easy process. Boiling will remove some of it, but carbon filtration works better and more thoroughly. Activated carbon water filters are so popular for drinking water now that they can be found in many grocery stores as well as big box retailers or specialty stores. Just follow the directions on how to use the activated carbon filter for drinking water and you will have great dechlorinated water for brewing as well.

Most of the recipes in this book can be made perfectly with the typical municipal water supply. If your supply is unacceptable, use bottled spring water. If a recipe within this book specifically calls for a necessary water adjustment, it will be clearly marked within the recipe section.

Yeast

Ale and lager yeasts are both from the greater family with the fancy Latin name, *Saccharomyces cerevisiae*. Yeast is technically a fungus (that doesn't sound all that appetizing, does it?). The way yeast cells grow healthy and multiply is by eating sugar, excreting alcohol, and burping CO_2 (come to think of it, that doesn't sound very appetizing either!). This is the crass but easy explanation of the fermentation process.

When it comes to extreme beers, very few things equal the extreme nature of the spontaneously fermented lambic ales of Belgium. These beers hearken back to a time when all beers contained microorganisms, that could make them tart and acidic. Louis Pasteur's research on pasteurization showed brewers how to eliminate these wort-spoiling microbes. With this subtraction by elimination, beer changed and began to more closely resemble the beers we consume today. The lambic family of beers remains a remnant of these pre-Pasteur beers, and the method of producing lambics is now a protected appellation. This appellation requires that lambic wort be made from no less than 30 percent unmalted barley and it must undergo spontaneous fermentation for the production of alcohol in the finished beer.

HISTORICAL NOTE

Louis Pasteur

Man has been making beer since the Dark Ages. But it wasn't until the mid-1800s that Louis Pasteur discovered that yeast, a tiny organism, is what causes fermentation. He also discovered that wild yeast and bacteria are what cause beer to spoil. An emphasis on clean brewing practices was born out of his studies.

A healthy yeast head on a fermenting batch of ale

Conclusion

This simple overview of the ingredients and brewing process is the framework from which all recipes in this book will be executed. Extreme beers are beers with nontraditional ingredients or traditional ingredients added in exaggerated amounts. Most of the recipes in this book are extreme to one degree or another (more than a few are extreme in both ways). While making an extreme beer might add a step (or three) to the process, believe me when I say that if the brewing process outlined in this chapter makes sense, then the additional steps that have been added for certain brews will be just as easy to comprehend and perform. Making good beer is a skill. Making exceptional beer is an art form. While you may not be ready to wear a beret just yet, the goal here is to make you an artist in no time.

"Brewing evokes something deep-seeded and primal in all of us who call ourselves brewers. Extreme brewing causes us to step away from an age-old ritual and start on a new path into uncharted territory. Although this new path can be challenging, the rewards far outweigh the ends of a conventional brew day."

Mike Gerhart,
Dogfish Head Brewings & Eats

CHAPTER 2

Equipping Your Home Brewery

IN HOMEBREWING, as in any hobby, the process can be as simple or as complicated as you make it. Of course, the more complicated you decide to make the process, the more equipment you will need. By focusing on recipes that call for malt extract as the malt sugar source, the full-scale mashing step can be skipped. Eliminating this step will save you not only time on your brew day, but also money, as you won't need to purchase the necessary mashing equipment.

Another factor that will determine how much equipment you'll need is how often you're planning to brew. Most of the recipes in this book are for ales. Ales usually take a shorter time to make than lagers. Since so many of these recipes are for beers that are stronger than the average commercial varieties, they require extended fermenting and conditioning time. The actual time it takes to brew a batch of beer is fewer than four hours. However, with fermentation, aging, bottling, and bottle-conditioning (the time required to build up the desired level of carbonation in the bottle), there will be a turnaround time of about a month before all of your equipment is freed up to brew the next batch. If you plan to brew more frequently than this, you will need an extra carboy or two, extra bottles, and at least twice as much storage space.

WHERE TO BUY EQUIPMENT

There are so many more options for where to purchase your home-brewing equipment today than there were twenty years ago. The most common sources are local homebrewing and wine-making shops. Check online for one near you. Another option is to shop through mail catalog stores. A number of these sources are listed in the Resource section of this book. For the novice brewer, I highly recommend purchasing the equipment and the ingredients for your first few brews from a local homebrew shop. There are several reasons that this is preferable to the online or mail route. The biggest benefit is having the knowledge of an expert at your disposal. The people who run these shops are almost all passionate, seasoned homebrewers themselves. They know how to walk a novice through the steps of brewing and are usually amenable to follow-up questions that you might have as you make your beer. Another advantage is that you get to touch and feel the equipment you need before committing to purchasing it. Be sure to take your time when you go to make your homebrew purchases; ask the shop worker to explain the use of every single piece of equipment and don't be afraid to take notes on the spot. Assuming you are buying a brewpot and not just using something you already own for cooking, you will be spending several hundred dollars on all the equipment. For that kind of invest-

A clean carboy is essential to homebrewing; sterilize your carboy prior to use by agitating with sanitizer and warm water.

ment, the storekeeper should be very willing to walk you through the use and cleaning of each piece of equipment. The other bonus to buying your equipment and ingredients locally is that you can analyze the condition and quality of everything before committing to a purchase. This is especially critical when it comes to buying ingredients. Freshness is key and you don't want to be stuck making beer with old barley, hops, or yeast. After you have a few batches under your belt and you're comfortable with the use of ingredients and equipment, you may choose to use the online and catalog options—but again, it's never a bad idea to have the resources of an expert local homebrewer at your disposal.

SANITIZING YOUR EQUIPMENT

While not a piece of homebrewing equipment per se, what you use to sanitize with and how you do it are major factors in determining the drinkability of your beer. Sanitizing should be the first thing you do when you bring home your new equipment, as countless people most likely have already handled it. The cheapest and most readily available sanitizing agent is common bleach. All that's needed is 1 tablespoon (15 ml) of bleach per gallon (3.8 L) of water to sanitize your equipment. Bleach is so strong that it's important to make sure any surface you clean with it that will come into contact with the beer has been well flushed with clean, hot water. If any bleach residue is left behind it can change the taste of your beer and even kill the yeast and prevent fermentation. Bleach should also not be used on stainless steel. There are several different prepackaged sanitizing agents available at most supply sources that are equally useful and more forgiving than bleach. Some of these are no-rinse cleansers that can help reduce the possible contamination from rinse water.

BASIC EQUIPMENT

Chapter three will take you through the step-by-step process of brewing a batch of beer. For the sake of continuity, the equipment you'll need to brew with is listed in the same order as it is used in chapter 3: Making Your First Batch of Beer, (page 45).

> "A few years ago, we began brewing some 'extreme' beers at Allagash. Some of our drinkers were quick to point out that these beers were a departure from the Belgian styles that we had always brewed. We believe that these beers fit very well into the Belgian beer tradition. They may not follow the stricter style guidelines of beers like our white, but we see Belgian beers as being experimental, in many ways, by their very nature."
>
> Rob Tod,
> Allagash Brewing Company

All the equipment you will need to take your beer from the brewpot, through fermentation and into the bottle: **A** stirring spoon, **B** brewpot, **C** thermometer, **D** specialty grain bag, **E** can opener, **F** whole leaf hop bag, **G** hydrometer and test vial, **H** funnel, **I** carboy with stopper and airlock on top, **J** siphon setup, **K** bottle caps, **L** capper, **M** bottle brush, **N** bottling bucket, **O** bottle tree with bottles, and **P** bottle filler

Stirring Spoon

You will want to have a good long spoon made from either stainless steel or rigid, unmeltable plastic. Wood is all right to use during the boil, but remember that wood is porous and an excellent home for beer-spoiling bacteria. The design of the spoon should be as simple as possible. An ornate, grooved spoon or one stamped with a funky design might look nice, but any grooves, nooks, or crannies are only going to make sanitization that much more difficult. The length of the handle is most easily determined by considering the height of the brewpot's sidewall. The handle of the spoon should be a good foot longer than the pot's height. A well-brewed beer is one that's made with a vigorous boil. There is nothing worse than being burned by the splash of boiling beer that can occur when you are adding hops or other ingredients to the boil. There is less chance of this happening if your stirring spoon has a nice long handle.

Brewpot

Of all the equipment you'll need for homebrewing, the brewpot may be the most expensive. However, trying to go the cheap route for this particular tool can adversely affect the quality of your beer. That said, there are ways to save some money on this investment. The stainless steel brewpots found in homebrew supply stores are no different from those used in commercial restaurant kitchens. Start scouring used-restaurant supply stores (found in every mid-to-large city) or restaurant auctions for an appropriately sized pot. If you spend a little energy hunting for a simple, smooth, used stainless steel brewpot you can easily save over 50 percent. When shopping, look for an oversized, 100 percent stainless steel pot. You will be brewing 5 gallon (19 L) batches, but it's important to have plenty of headroom for accommodating extra ingredients and a vigorous boil. A 7 or 8 gallon (26 or 30 L) pot is ideal. You might be tempted to use inexpensive, porcelain-covered steel or aluminum pots, but don't. With all of the stirring required in making good beer, it's inevitable that the porcelain will eventually chip and the now-exposed cheaper steel will rust and contribute a metallic taste and possibly contaminate your beer.

Thermometer

While you may be tempted to buy a digital-readout probe thermometer at a homebrew supply shop, an inexpensive glass thermometer purchased at any super-market is just as effective. In my experience, the digital ones can be complicated to use and lose calibration easily. Also, home-cooking thermometers don't float and tend to be sturdier. You need the thermometer for properly steeping specialty grains, chilling the beer for appropriate yeast-pitching temperatures, and monitoring fermentation temperatures, so it's really not a good idea to skimp on a simple piece of equipment that is this critical. A wide range of easy to use and effective thermometers have appeared in recent years, including a liquid crystal style that attaches to the outside of the vessel and clip-on dial thermometers for the brew pot.

Specialty Grain Bag

Specialty grain bags are the extreme brewer's best friend. They are little cheesecloth or nylon bags that hold about 1 pound (455 g) or so of specialty grains. Specialty grains can be steeped without a bag, but then you'll need to use a tight colander or some other means of straining out the barley solids after the steeping is complete. It's much easier to use these inexpensive bags that can be found in any good homebrew supply source. Look for the kind that has a drawstring closure on the top to keep the grains from floating out. Basically, they're like giant tea bags and you will probably get a few uses out of one drawstring bag before it falls apart. If these aren't available, make sure the bag is big enough to hold the grain needed for the recipe and

"For me, extreme brewing is taking inspiration from the brewers of Belgium and putting my own unique twist on their Old-World traditions. It is also thinking outside the box to create and develop unique flavors."

Vinnie Cilurzo,
Russian River Brewing Company

that there's enough material left at the top of the bag to tightly knot and seal. The cheesecloth bags are cheap enough that it won't be too painful to your wallet to use them once and throw them out.

You may also use the specialty grain bags to occasionally hold whole-leaf hops. Hop pellets break into small particles easily enough that they can be added freely to the boil or fermented when the recipes calls for them. Whole-leaf hops, however, can get pretty messy and block the flow of beer from the brewpot to the carboy or from the carboy to the bottling bucket. By packing the whole-leaf hops into a cheesecloth sack, they will be much easier to use, remove from the beer, and dispose of. It is important not to pack the sacks too tightly as the hops will expand when wet. To fully absorb the goodness of the hops the whole sack should be soaked through by the beer.

Can Opener

A basic can opener will be needed to open the cans of malt extract.

Hydrometer and Test Vial

This is one of the most critical tools for properly making beer at home. A hydrometer measures the amount of sugar in the beer by measuring the specific gravity. It bobs in a test vial and is marked along its neck in a similar way that a thermometer is marked. As the yeast eats the sugars and converts them to alcohol, there will be fewer sugars in the solution, which lowers the specific gravity of the beer. The higher the specific gravity of the beer, the higher the hydrometer floats in the vial. The lower the specific gravity, the deeper the hydrometer will be submerged in the beer. The hydrometer is used on brew day to make sure that the original target specific gravity has been hit. It's also used to test the beer as it ferments so that you will know when it hits the desired final specific gravity. You are best off buying a hydrometer from a trusted homebrew supply source. Make sure it's properly calibrated for testing beer, as different hydrometers are used in different industries. The test vial can be purchased either with or separately from the hydrometer. As the hydrometer is made of glass, it's best to store it within the vial somewhere safe when it's not in use. While you can get glass vials, I recommend getting one made from food-grade plastic as the glass vials can break pretty easily as well.

Funnel

The funnel is used to transfer the beer from the brewpot to the glass carboy at the end of your brew day. It's best to use a funnel with a thin enough neck to sit comfortably and securely into the top opening of your carboy. A good funnel is made of food-grade plastic and is usually between 8 inches (20.3 cm) and 1 foot (30.5 cm) in diameter at its widest point.

Carboy

Using a glass carboy for fermentation is a simple yet worthwhile upgrade to invest in. Most turnkey, start-up homebrew kits come with two food-grade 5- to 8-gallon (19 to 30 L) buckets for fermenting and another one for bottling. The plastic fermenters work fine but can be difficult to clean as they have a flat bottom and the plastic is usually more porous than a glass carboy. Rarely, when using ingredients that are larger than the opening of the carboy, plastic buckets actually work better because of their large openings. At a minimum, the carboy should be large enough to yield 5 gallon (19 L) batches though it's really best to use a 6- or 6½-gallon (23 or 25 L) glass carboy so that there is plenty of space in the top for vigorously fermenting strong batches of beer. Many types of plastic are permeable by oxygen. However, a newer type of carboy made from a plastic called PET (polyethylene terephthalate) has recently been introduced to the homebrewer. PET plastic is acceptable for homebrewing as it's not permeable by oxygen. PET carboys are lightweight (1½ pounds [680 g] versus over 14 pounds [6.3 kg] for a 6½-gallon [25 L] carboy), they won't break, and they have a larger opening than glass carboys. Before brewing, fill your carboy with water poured from a gallon jug so that you can use tape to mark the targeted 5-gallon (19 L) point on the outside of the carboy. The more sugar added during fermentation, whether fruit purée, brown sugar, or anything else, the more the yeast will multiply and the more space you'll need to accommodate yeast growth and the additional ingredients themselves.

Whether you use a bucket or a carboy for primary fermentation, you'll need a glass or PET plastic carboy, sized to your batch of beer,

While not necessary, it's nice to have two carboys so that you can transfer the beer out of the first one and let it age a bit in the second. The primary fermenting carboy will have a lot of proteins and spent yeast cells that will settle to the bottom after fermentation. It helps to remove the beer from these solids if you plan to age it for an extended period of time before bottling.

A dark, well-sealed bottle
protects the beer from sunlight.

(usually 5 gallons [19 L]) if you plan to secondary ferment. Secondary fermentation is more about storing the beer for dry hopping and clarification than about actual fermentation. This is also a good way to store your beer if you find you don't have time to bottle it. I like to get the beer out of the bucket within two weeks of the start of fermentation. The beer can be racked to a secondary fermentation vessel any time after most of the fermentation has been completed (4 to 7 days after start of fermentation). Visually, you'll notice the foam head of an ale will star to fall, or, if you use a hydrometer, you'll notice the gravity has dropped more than ¾ of the way from starting to finish gravity. After racking the beer to the carboy and adding any dry hops, if needed, the carboy should be topped off with water to be within 4 inches (10 cm) of the top to reduce oxidation. Little air will be left at the top of the carboy. A stopper and airlock must be fitted to the carboy to keep it from getting contaminated and releasing any CO_2.

Stopper and Airlock

For most of the buckets designed for homebrewing, you will need only an airlock. The bucket lid will come with a hole that is fitted with a rubber gasket into which the airlock will fit snuggly. Some buckets come with a large hole that requires a stopper, and all carboys require a stopper. The rubber stopper has a similar hole on top and is sized to fit tightly in the neck of a standard carboy. There are a few common designs for airlocks that can be bought from any homebrew supply source; they all work well and are around the same price. The airlock allows the beer to ferment safely, without exposing it to any potential airborne contaminants. As the yeast eats the sugars and converts them to alcohol, the byproduct, CO_2, needs to escape. If the fermenter was sealed, the gas would have nowhere to go and the pressure build-up would eventually break the fermenter. The airlock has space for water within its chamber so that the gas can bubble through without exposing the beer in the fermenter to air. You can also use grain alcohol or vodka in the airlock to make sure the liquid can't grow bacteria, but boiled or distilled sterile water works fine, too.

Siphon Setup

This setup will be used to transfer the beer from the carboy into the bottling bucket and then from the bottling bucket into bottles. Look for food-grade, 3/8-inch (1 cm) OD racking cane and 5/16-inch (8 mm) or 3/8-inch (1 cm) tubing (check your homebrew supply source) and make sure it's long enough to do the job properly. It needs to be capable of running from the bottom of a carboy, out the top, and down into the bottom of another carboy with a bit of room to spare. Six or seven feet (1.8 or 2.1 m) of hosing should suffice. There is a lot of surface area inside this piece of hose, so make sure it's sufficiently flushed out after using it and well sanitized before using it again. The racking cane should have a footing to keep from pulling sediment from the bottom.

Bottle Caps

Homebrew supply sources offer a few different options for bottle caps. The styles that have a thin, porous, oxygen-scavenging layer on the inside cost a bit more but are worth the price. They will absorb a good amount of the oxygen present in the bottleneck (between the cap and the top of the beer itself), which will improve the taste and shelf life of your beer. If there is a decent-sized craft brewery near you, it can't hurt to ask if they have any extra bottle caps they aren't using and may be willing to part with. Oftentimes, when a brewery changes its cap artwork, they'll end up with cases of the old design that they're willing to part with, sometimes for free. Make sure the caps are sterilized in a solution of hot water just before using them.

Capper

There are two standard options for homebrew cappers and both work fine. The cheaper option is the double-lever, hand-held model that gets placed over the top of the bottle when being used. You have to manually hold the cap on the top of the bottle when using this style capper. The more expensive type sits on a little platform and uses a magnet to hold the cap in place. You then place the beer-filled

While there are a number of bottle cappers available, this style is simple and easy to use.

bottle on the center of the platform and pull a lever down to crimp the cap onto the top of the bottle. The cheaper style involves a bit more elbow grease and isn't quite as durable as the second option, but unless you are bottling every day, it should hold up just fine.

Bottle Brushes

These simple brushes are sized to fit into the necks of bottles so that you can properly clean them out before using them again. Whether you use a brush or not, it's wise to wash out every bottle of beer that you plan to fill with homebrew and then store them in a case box upside down. This will prevent them from getting really cruddy on the bottom. You may want to buy a bottle rinser, which is a device that attaches to most sink spouts and shoots a jet of water into the empty bottle. They don't cost much and are easier to use than a bottle brush, but will work only if your bottles were well rinsed after their last use.

Bottling Bucket

The standard bottling bucket holds at least 5 gallons (19 L) of beer and comes with a plastic valve near its base to which the siphon setup is secured for bottling. You will be filling this bucket with the beer from your carboy just before bottling. Before adding the beer to the bucket, add your sterile-water-diluted priming sugar to ensure predictable carbonation within each bottle. Making sure the whole setup is completely sanitized before use is critical. Don't forget to breakdown the screw-on valve at the base of the bottling bucket and soak all of the parts in sanitizing solution before and after using them.

A specially designed bottle rinser is indispensable for sanitizing your bottles.

Bottle Tree

You can make a bottle tree yourself but they don't cost that much to buy from a homebrew supply sources and they make the bottling process a lot more organized, sanitary, and manageable. As their name suggests, they look like little trees with bare branches that are angled upwards. Once the bottles are cleaned, you place them bottle-neck down on the bottle tree. This allows them to drip dry before bottling and it keeps them in a clean, easy-to-access place. Many bottle trees have a swivel base so you can spin them and pluck the bottles off as needed. Make sure that the branches of the tree have been wiped down with sanitizer prior to bottling as they will be in contact with the inside of your bottles.

Bottles

With so many commercial breweries bottling their beer in either clear or green glass for aesthetic purposes, most people assume they are as good an option as old-fashioned brown bottles. This is simply not true. Both green and clear glass allow light to get through the bottle, potentially damaging the beer. Big breweries use preserva-tives to maximize the shelf life of their beer but because homebrew is made with all natural ingredients, it's more susceptible to light damage, specifically, a skunky aroma. Therefore, you should always use brown glass.

The most standard size of brown bottle is the 12-ounce (355 ml) longneck favored by so many packaging craft breweries. They are

DIY Bottle Dryer

A HOMEMADE BOTTLE dryer can be made using a piece of 2˝x 10˝(5.1 x 25.4 cm) or 2˝x 12˝ (5.1 x 30.5 cm) lumber, and 18˝ to 24˝ (45.7 to 61 cm)-long as a base, with wood pegs or stain-less steel nails fitted in the wood. The wood should be painted or varnished to make cleaning easier and to prevent it from becom-ing contaminated with bacteria. Elevating the long side about 1 inch (2.5 cm) would allow water from the bottles to drain to one side and be caught by a towel that has been placed under the dryer.

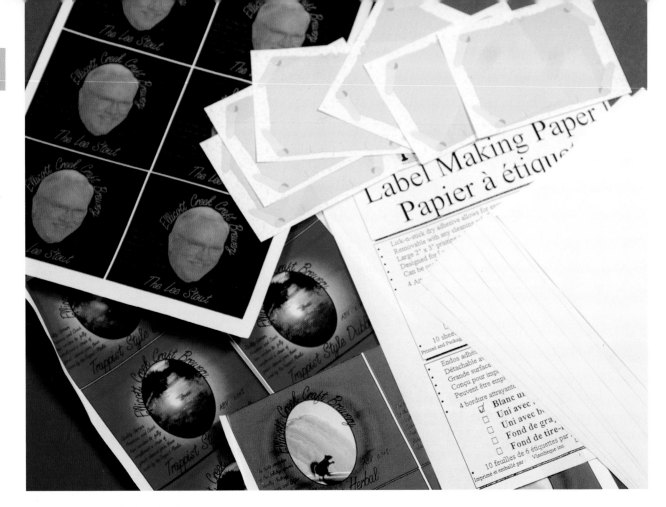

Many resources can be found online to create personalized beer labels at home. See the Resources section on page 217.

easy to find and easy to use. Be sure to use a bottle that requires a bottle opener as opposed to a twist-off style. The pop-top option gives a much better seal to prevent flat-beer, oxidation, and potentially spoiled beer. Many craft breweries and homebrewers also package in 22-ounce (630-ml) "bomber" bottles or 750 ml Champagne bottles. They make for a more impressive presentation and are ideally sized for sharing with friends over a meal. More importantly, they hold roughly twice as much beer as a standard 12-ounce (355-ml) bottle, which means you'll be cleaning, filling, and capping half as many bottles needed for a 5-gallon (19-L) batch. Make sure they all take a standard crown cap, some of the European bottles won't. A 5-gallon (19-L) batch will yield slightly more than two cases, or fifty to fifty-five 12-ounce (355-ml) bottles. It's a good idea to clean a few extra bottles to have on hand as you never know when one might slip and break or when your dog might slobber over the top of one and render it unsanitary.

Bottle Filler

Many bottling buckets have a simple valve near the bottom of the sidewall that can either be used alone for bottling or connected to the hose of the siphon setup and bottle filler. The hose and bottle filler method is better. The bottle filler is a rigid food-grade plastic tube that has a valve at the bottom that will stop and start the filling action when it's depressed against the bottom of the bottle. This method allows the bottle to be filled from the bottom up, which is important. This process helps to evacuate unwanted air from the bottle that can lead to oxidation and possible spoilage.

THE FINISHING TOUCH

While it isn't necessary to label your bottles of homebrew, it is fun, easy, and offers the opportunity to further differentiate the beer that you have proudly made from commercial brews.

The easiest way to make quality labels is to use colored paper personalized with your own artwork and verbiage, run it off from your home printer. Once the artwork is the right size, you should be able to fit six or eight labels on a standard 8½ x 11-inch (21.6 x 27.9 cm) piece of paper. After the labels have been printed, lay them out on newspaper in a well-ventilated area. Spray the front with a film of clear polyurethane. This will protect the label and prevent the artwork from bleeding once the bottle becomes wet. After they're dry, cut out the individual labels and affix them to the clean, finished bottles of homebrew with strong glue.

Once you have purchased all the necessary equipment, take some time to really familiarize yourself with the function of each item before your first brew day. It's only natural to be a bit anxious as you begin the first batch so it's best not to add to this by trying to learn about the equipment at the same time that your beer is boiling. It's a good idea to set each piece of equipment up in the actual order in which it will be used, as this will cut down on potential confusion. Focus on keeping everything as simple (and sanitized) as possible and you'll be well on your way to producing your first batch of extremely enjoyable, extreme beer.

Some homebrewers use bottles that still have labels of a big commercial brewer on them. Compared to a clean, unmarked bottle, or those with a home-made label, the bottles that were never cleaned off usually aren't as good. Maybe some fraction of this reality is perception, but the individual who takes the time to personalize and enhance his or her bottle artwork usually takes more effort to personalize and enhance the quality of the beer within that bottle.

Making Your First Batch of Beer

THERE ARE TWO PARTS to any successful beer recipe. This first part lists the ingredients needed to brew the highest-quality beer. The second is the process—the sequence of steps you must take to successfully make a particular beer. This chapter will cover the finer points of both steps. Don't expect your first batch to go perfectly. Though it's perfectly natural to have a little anxiety, it's important to realize that mistakes do happen. But if you take the time to develop a plan that includes gathering ingredients and equipment, and then thoroughly read the process before beginning, the odds are really good that you'll be enjoying the fruits of your labor in no time flat. If you are brewing with a friend, use the time it takes to sip a pint together to review the forthcoming day's brew and locate ingredients and equipment.

Whether it's a small batch produced at home or an enormous batch made at a commercial brewery, the actual brewing of the beer takes only a small fraction of the time it takes to ferment and age, which can be anywhere from a week to several months. Ales usually ferment in half the time that lagers do, but the stronger the beer (with more fermentable sugars available for the yeast to eat), the longer it will take to ferment and mature before it's at its optimal quality. You will move your beer into primary fermentation on the same day it is brewed.

A GOOD CARPENTER
HAS ALL OF HIS TOOLS READY

The first thing to do on brew day is review your equipment and ingredients. Make sure the equipment is clean and in working order and that all of your ingredients are fresh.

Equipment

Most equipment required to brew beer comes with the turnkey homebrew kits that are sold online or at a neighborhood homebrew supply store. Kits usually include a plastic bucket for fermenting and bottling, as well as other tools. The only upgrades I suggest are a glass carboy, specialty grain sacks, and a bottle tree. The glass carboy will allow you to more easily see how well your beer is fermenting, and to know when it is done. Also, glass is a lot easier to clean and has less of a chance of contamination than plastic. The most common sizes of glass carboys used in homebrewing are 5 and 6 gallons (19 and 23 L) and I recommend buying the 6-gallon (23 L) size. While the recipes outlined in this book are designed to yield 5 gallons (19 L) of beer, having a carboy with extra space is a good idea, particularly when brewing strong beers or beers with fruit and other sugars added during fermentation. The extra space will accommodate the extra yeast growth and vigorous fermentation that takes place when the additional ingredients are introduced, reducing the chance that the beer will ferment out the top of the vessel. Upgrading to specialty grains will allow you to make more diverse styles of beer than if you brewed with extract alone. And, finally, a bottle tree is worth having because it offers a more convenient and sanitary way to prepare and stage your bottles for when the beer is ready to be packaged.

Ingredients

This particular recipe illustrates the extent to which additional sugars can add to the alcohol content and complexity of beer. This batch contains malt extract, steeped specialty grains, hops, water, yeast, Irish moss (a clarifying agent), and the following sugars: Belgian candi (beet sugar), maple, molasses, and brown sugar.

- Check your malt extract syrup cans for a date to make sure they were canned within the last twelve months. Expiration dates are not clearly marked on all cans. Modern malt extract production gives it a fairly long shelf life, but the malt will darken over time. This may become a problem when making a light-colored beer.
- Check the hop pellets to make sure they are fresh and more green than brown. They should disintegrate between the thumb and finger only with great effort. If they are spongy or crumble easily, they are not at their peak. Hops are grown on trellises and are dependant on an ideal growing climate for their quality. Different varieties will contribute different levels of taste and aroma. They are harvested each fall, then processed and shipped. Some hop varieties store better than others so check with your supplier to determine quality and freshness.

"Extreme brewing is like driving 90 mph on a winding road that you've driven a million times before—except it's nighttime and raining, your headlights have burned out, and the Department of Transportation has removed all of the guardrails to upgrade them."

Bryan Selders,
Dogfish Head Craft Brewery

All the necessary ingredients for brewing your first batch of beer. From left to right:

- **A.** gypsum
- **B.** crushed crystal malt
- **C.** malt extract
- **D.** Cluster hop pellets
- **E.** Northern Brewer hop pellets
- **F.** molasses
- **G.** brown sugar
- **H.** Belgiun candi sugar
- **I.** Irish moss
- **J.** Kent Goldings Hops
- **K.** yeast
- **L.** maple syrup
- **M.** priming sugar

SANITATION

The importance of sanitation cannot be overemphasized; it is the single biggest factor between producing a drinkable beer and one that must be dumped. Yeast is not the only microorganism that likes to eat sugar; bacteria like to eat it too. Like yeast, certain kinds of bacteria will multiply very quickly in a sugar-rich environment. They can overwhelm the yeast and rapidly make your beer sour and undrinkable. Sanitize your equipment by scrubbing the surface of everything with clean water and a cleaning agent such as B-Brite, C-Brite, Eazy Clean or Easy Alkaline (some of the commercial brands developed for brewers), or if clean, simply use Star San or Iodophor. It's always better to err on the side of cleaning too much as opposed to not cleaning enough.

READING THE RECIPE

Starting and final specific gravity and International Bittering Units (IBUs) are key terms that you will see listed at the bottom of each recipe in this book. These measurements have a great effect on the outcome of your finished brew as well as the final alcohol content by volume.

E-Brew

WHEN CREATING a recipe, don't be afraid to write down every step of the process, including when to add what to what. In the last ten years, some great resources have materialized on the Internet to help with this process. The Resources section of this book lists a number of websites that offer great templates for homebrew recipes where you can plug in the specific ingredients and target alcohol content of your recipe. Some of the programs will even tell you how much more specific gravity will come from adding different sugars and how much more bitterness (IBUs) can be achieved by adding a certain quantity of hops.

Gravity

Gravity is the measurement of how much sugar is in your wort. You measure gravity by using a hydrometer. Before the yeast converts the sugar into alcohol, the gravity will be very high. Once the yeast has done its job and there is very little sugar left, the gravity will be low. The gravity before fermenting is called initial, or starting gravity and the hydrometer will bob high in its test vial at this point. When you put your finished beer into a clean test vial after fermentation, the hydrometer will sink deep into the liquid. This final measurement is called the terminal, or final gravity. Use the alcohol scale on your hydrometer. Subtract your end reading from your initial reading to get your final alcohol content.

$$\text{Alcohol by volume} = \frac{\text{Original gravity}}{0.75}$$

International Bittering Units

IBUs are the measured units that brewers use to gauge the level of hop bitterness in beers. Different hops have different alpha acid levels; the more alpha acids a variety of hops has, the more bitterness they will impart on the beer. True bitterness can only be realized by boiling the hops. When you dry hop a beer, or add hops postboil, you will be adding to the hop aroma but not actually upping the actual IBUs or bitterness.

Gravity and IBU utilization are really the only technical concepts that move the homebrewing experience beyond the normal cooking procedures that any good chef would be faced with in the kitchen. They are not difficult to master and once you are comfortable with them you are on the way to being a very competent brewer.

BROWN ALE INGREDIENTS

Preboil

1/2 pound (225 g) crystal-crushed
   specialty grain

Boil

6.6 pounds (3k g) light liquid malt extract
   or 5 pounds (2.25 kg) dry malt extract
   (65 minutes)

1 ounce (28 g) Northern Brewer
   hop pellets *(60 minutes)*

1 pound (455 g) Belgiun candi sugar
   (30 minutes)

1/2 ounce (14 g) Cluster hop pellets
   (30 minutes)

1 teaspoon (5 g) Irish moss *(20 minutes)*

8 ounces (225 g) brown sugar
   (15minutes)

8 ounces (340 ml) molasses *(15 minutes)*

1 ounce (28 g) whole leaf Goldings hops
   (10 minutes)

Fermentation

1 vial or slap pack of American Ale Yeast
   sized for a 5-gallon (19 L) batch; Safale
   US-05; White Labs WLP001; or
   Wyeast 1056

8 to10 ounces (340–425 ml) maple
   syrup *(2 to3 days into fermentation)*

5 ounces (140 g) priming sugar

Bottling

NOTE: *All the ingredients listed in the recipes in
this book are organized by the order in which they
are called for in the process, and the time they should
be added to the recipe from pre-boil tea to bottling.
The first step is to add the ingredients listed to create
the pre-boil tea. (See step B, page 51.) Begin to add
the ingredients listed under "boil" from the time the
boil begins. The remaining time notations indicate
fermentation time, dry hopping, and bottling time.*

BREWING STEP-BY-STEP
A-to-Z Brown Ale

It's now time to start brewing the virgin batch. The pilot brew being made is called A-to-Z Brown Ale. Although the beer will be complex, the brewing process is not—without the incremental addition of exotic sugars it would be a relatively generic brown ale. I promise, if you can drink a beer, you can make this beer. There are twenty-six letters in the alphabet and there are twenty-six steps in brewing this beer, hence the name.

To enhance the complexity and alcohol content of this brew, you'll be adding a number of easy-to-find sugars and a small amount of specialty grains before the actual boil. Other than these simple grain and sugar additions, the recipe and process for making this beer are identical to those you would use for a batch of homebrew made strictly from unhopped malt extract.

An additional note regarding ingredient quantities: Although liquid measurements are typically given in gallons (and liters), liquid malt extract usually comes in large containers that are weighed as pounds (and kilograms). When a recipe calls for a number of pounds (or kilograms) for a liquid ingredient, it is usually referring to the size of the container that it comes in.

A. Heat the water for use in the brewing process.

Some of the older homebrewing books recommend boiling the malt extract in 1 1/2 gallons (5.7 L) of water, but this ratio makes for syrupy wort (prefermented beer) that can result in unwanted color due to caramelization. Ideally, wort should be thin. The secret is to use a bigger pot—something stainless steel that can hold at least 5 gallons (19 L). The goal is to start with 5 gallons (19 L) of wort and end up with about 4 1/2 gallons (17 L) after the normal evaporation rate during a standard one-hour boil. After adding 4 1/2 gallons (17 L) of cold water to the brewpot, load the crushed crystal specialty grains into the grain bag; knot the opening at the top and place in the cold water. Place the pot on the stove burner and turn burner on high.

B. Steep the specialty grains to make preboil tea.

As the water temperature increases, your specialty grains' sugars and flavors will start to dissolve. This will give the beer more complexity and depth. Let the grains steep in the brewpot until the water temperature rises to 170°F (77°C). Occasionally move the grain bag up and down as you would when using a tea bag to make tea. This will help extract more of the flavors and sugars out of the grains.

A. Load the specialty grains into the grain bag.

B. Place the grain bag into the brewpot.

C. Add the malt extract to the boil pot.

C. Add the malt extract.

When the water temperature rises to 170°F (77°C), pull the grain bag out of the brewpot using your stirring spoon, and hold it directly above the pot to let most of the water drain from the bag. Do not squeeze the excess water from the grain bag or allow the water temperature to rise above 170°F (77°C) before removing the grain, as these actions will introduce too many tannins into your beer. Next, remove the pot from the heat, add the malt extract to the brewpot, and thoroughly stir to make sure all the malt dissolves. If any malt is left sticking to the bottom of the pot it has the potential to burn or scorch. Liquid malt extract is thick and syrupy, so don't be afraid to dip your can of nearly empty extract into the wort and swirl the hot liquid around inside. (Make sure the can is fairly clean before submerging it in the wort but remember that the boiling process itself will sterilize the wort.) This will bring the extract clinging to the inside walls of the can into the liquid solution. Dump all the liquid in the can back into the brewpot. Repeat as needed.

D. Return to heat and stir occasionally as the wort comes to a boil.

This will help to break down any clumps of extract that would add unwanted color and reduce the amount of available sugars. Liquid malt extract will cling to the bottom of the pot and may be scorched; removing the pot from the heat and stirring will prevent this from happening.

E. Once the wort begins to boil, add a few hop pellets to the boiling liquid. An antifoam agent may also be added.

This will help reduce the chance of a boil over.

Because homebrewers often try to make their beers in smaller pots, they have less-than-ideal headspace to allow for a vigorous boil. A vigorous boil means better hop utilization and better breakdown of all of the added sugars. A bigger brewpot helps.

F. Pour the hop pellets into the boiling wort.

F. Add the Northern Brewer hop pellets to the brewpot after boiling for 5 minutes.

Stir the boiling wort to help break down the hop pellets and any chunks of malt extract that may have formed. Start timing your 60-minute boil at this hop addition.

G. Add candi sugar and the cluster hop pellets.

Add the Belgian candi (beet) sugar, as this will take the longest time to dilute into the wort, 30 minutes into the boil. Stir for a couple of minutes until there are no more chunks at the bottom of your brewpot. Add the cluster hop pellets.

H. Add Irish moss.

Add the Irish moss, which will act as a clarifying agent for the beer, 40 minutes into the boil.

I. Add more sugars.

Add the brown sugar and molasses 45 minutes into the boil. Stir for a couple of minutes.

J. Add the whole-leaf Goldings hops.

Stuff the whole-leaf Goldings hops into the hop bag and tie off the top. It helps to put a heavy knife or spoon in the bag as the extra weight will keep the bag submerged in the boiling liquid. Just don't forget about your silverware when throwing out the used hop bag at the end of the brew! Submerge the bag of hops into your brewpot 50 minutes into the boil.

G. Add brown sugar and molasses to the boil.

K. Shut off the stove burner 60 minutes into the boil.

Remove pot from the heat source.

The brewpot in a cold water
bath in the sink

L. Create a whirlpool.

After a minute or so, stir the now-still wort clockwise with a sanitized stirring spoon until you build up a whirlpool effect. This action will help push some of the unwanted solids to the center and bottom of the brewpot. Stir the beer in this manner for 2 minutes and then let the pot sit for a bit.

M. Create a cooling water bath.

As the brewpot is cooling, fill your sink halfway with water and a few trays of ice. Assuming your sink is of ample size, it will act as a cold water bath to cool the beer before transferring it into the glass carboy and pitching the yeast. Carefully set the brewpot in the cold water and let it sit for 30 minutes or so. This is a good time to clean up the mess that is inevitable with homebrewing. Be careful not to clean near the brewpot. As the beer temperature drops below 180°F (82°C), it's capable of supporting bacterial growth and you don't want to risk contaminating it. Change water as needed to cool the brewpot. Put the brewpot in a cold water bath in the sink.

N. Transfer the beer.

You should calibrate your fermenter ahead of time by filling it with water poured from a gallon (3.8-L) container. This will you allow you to mark the exact 5-gallon (19 L) level on the outside of the bucket or carboy with tape or permanent marker. Prepare to transfer the beer from the brewpot to the carboy by putting the carboy on the floor in front of the sink. Put the funnel in the top of carboy. Once the beer temperature falls below 75°F (24°C), it's ready to be transferred. Pour the cooled wort into the carboy using a large funnel. Leave behind in the brewpot as many solids as possible that will have accumulated due to the whirlpool. Allow to splash and aerate the wort as it introduces yeast-friendly oxygen.

N. Pour the wort from the brewpot into the fermenter.

FERMENTING STEP-BY-STEP

O. **Dilute the beer to the correct gravity.**

Once the beer is in the fermenter, add cold water, if needed until the liquid volume of wort is 4^1/$_2$ gallons (18 L). Take a sample of the water-diluted wort and pour it into a sterilized hydrometer tube. Record your initial gravity and temperature before adding the yeast. The target initial gravity is 1.072. If higher than that, dilute the wort with a little more water. If lower, record by how much and add a few extra ounces (or grams) of maple syrup at the prescribed point a little later in fermentation.

P. **Pitch your yeast.**

Use your thermometer to make sure the beer's temperature is between 65°F and 72°F (18°C and 22°C)—the ideal temperature for fermenting most ales in a 5-gallon (19-L) batch. The yeast will most likely come from a vial or slap pack, and most homebrew yeast packs are already premeasured for this size batch. Be very mindful of sanitation during this step; if the yeast comes in contact with a speck of food or dirt at this point, it can quickly become tainted. If you were brewing a lager batch, the process would be similar, but the target yeast pitching and fermenting temperature would be 15°F and 20°F (−9° and −6°C) cooler.

Q. **Rock the baby.**

"Rock the baby" (or aerate) means to grab the top of the fermenter, lift it off-center, and twirl it back and forth. This will help to mix the yeast and air into the beer to ensure a good start to the fermentation process. Always exercise extreme caution when rocking a glass carboy.

R. **Seal the top of the carboy with a sterilized rubber stopper and airlock filled with sterile water.**

Check the beer each day. If you are having a strong, successful fermentation, you will have CO_2 bubbling through the airlock within 24 hours of pitching the yeast. You will also see a whitish, foamy yeast head forming on the top of your fermenting beer.

P. Read the hydrometer by bobbing it in a cylinder of beer.

S. Prepare beer for the maple syrup addition.

Take a sample of your fermenting beer after a couple of days of fermentation. Take its temperature and hydrometer reading. Once the beer is down to a gravity of about 1.040, you are ready for the last sugar addition.

T. Add the maple syrup.

It's best to use 100 percent real maple syrup as many of the popular store bought brands are cut with cheap corn syrup and artificial additives that might retard fermentation. Assuming it's coming from an unopened container, feel free to add the syrup to the fermenter directly from the container (make sure the container itself is free of dust or dirt that could get into the carboy and taint your beer). If the maple syrup has already been opened, dump the required amount plus an extra 2 ounces (60 ml) into 6 ounces (175 ml) of boiling water. This will sanitize the maple syrup and the extra quantity that you added will compensate for the water dilution. Dump the syrup into the carboy with the beer. With this introduction of new sugars, the beer should ferment vigorously for a few more days. You will notice that your airlock may bubble more briskly after adding the maple syrup. You may want to place a towel beneath the carboy in case a bit of yeasty foam runs out of the airlock and down the side.

U. Check the final gravity.

After a week or so, once the airlock has stopped bubbling for a few days and the beer looks a lot clearer, take another gravity reading with the hydrometer. The target final gravity is 1.010. The period from brew day to bottling should take just under three weeks.

V. Siphon the beer for bottling.

After the fermentation is complete, siphon the beer into the sterilized bottling bucket. Dump the corn sugar in 1 cup (235 ml) of boiling water. Stir until completely dissolved, then shut of your heat source.

W. Add the sugar water to the bottling bucket and gently stir with a sanitized stirring spoon.

The sugar water is heavier than the beer you've added it to, so you are stirring to make sure that it thoroughly dilutes into the beer. This final sugar addition will be your source of carbonation in the bottle. Remember, when yeast eats sugar and converts it to alcohol, the natural byproduct is CO_2. By introducing more sugar to the beer just before bottling, you will allow the beer to referment in the bottle. Since the CO_2 has nowhere to escape to, as it did through the airlock on top of the carboy, it goes into the solution and naturally carbonates your beer. Isn't Mother Nature awesome?

BOTTLING STEP-BY-STEP

X. Sanitize the bottles.

Sterilize your bottles using one of the sanitizing solutions. Twenty-two ounce (650 ml) bottles or Champagne bottles (750 ml) are ideal to use for homebrewing, as they are much bigger than the standard 12-ounce (355 ml) beer bottle, allowing you to package a batch of beer in half the amount of time. The recipe yields roughly two cases of beer, but have a few extra bottles clean and handy, as you never know when one might break or get dirty.

Y. Bottle the beer.

Fill bottles until the liquid content is halfway up the thin part of the neck and then cap with sterilized bottle caps. Once your bottles are filled and capped, find a safe, 70°F (21°C) space in which to store them.

Z. Store the bottled beer before drinking.

Your bottled beer will need to be stored at room temperature (70–72°F [21–22°C]) for a couple weeks to give the yeast a chance to referment and carbonate the bottles. After two weeks, throw a few bottles in the fridge for your next party and put the remaining bottles in a cool, dark place for aging. Since this beer has a targeted alcohol content of 9 percent by volume, it will age well. Be sure to date and label the bottles if you plan to have multiple batches of homebrew in your inventory at any given time.

Pop the top on a bottle of your A-to-Z Brown Ale and share it with a friend. Congrats, you've just completed your first batch of beer!

Y. Cap the beer while a friend fills the bottles.

Homebrewers enjoying the fruit of their labors

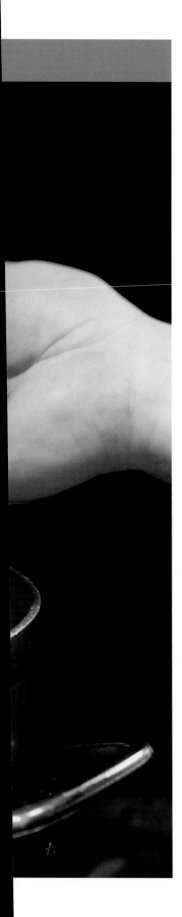

CHAPTER 4

Components of an Extreme Beer

ACCORDING TO THE Alcohol and Tobacco Tax and Trade Bureau (the branch of the federal government that regulates alcohol), beer is considered beer if it is fermented from a mixture of the following big-four ingredients: malt, hops, yeast, and water. Corn and rice are also typically included as brewing ingredients in commercial production because the big brewers are so fond of using these alternative and cheaper sources of carbohydrates. Corn and rice also have the advantage of thinning out the body, of the product to make the beer lighter. However, in addition to the aforementioned staples, there are many ingredients, such as fruits, sugars, spices, herbs, and wild yeast, which have been used in beer making for centuries. Thanks to the recent craft beer renaissance, they are once again finding favor with brewers as they add complexity and balance and offer endless creative possibilities.

There are a number of easy ways to make any ordinary beer more extreme by simply adjusting the amounts of barley and hops or altering the fermentation methods with specialty yeasts. Or, if you're feeling more adventurous, you can add fruits, herbs, and spices to the brew. Now that you have a good sense of how beer is made, it's time to discuss how to transform your homebrew from ordinary to extraordinary, from mundane to extreme.

TAKING STANDARD INGREDIENTS TO THE EXTREME

Malted Barley

Malted barley is the primary source of fermentable carbohydrate in all homebrews and commercial beers alike. Carbohydrates are first broken down into sugar components in the brewing process. Whether these sugars are accessed during brewing via malt extract syrup, dried powdered malt extract, or crushed malt is of minor importance in the context of extreme brewing. In general, the more malt and/or extract added to a 5-gallon (19-L) batch of beer, the more sugars will be present in the wort, and the more alcohol the batch will yield after fermentation. Darker malts tend to lend more flavor and color than do fermentable sugar. The easiest way to bump up the complexity of your homebrew is to incorporate crushed specialty barley grains to augment the use of malt extract. Color in malt is attained through the varying duration and temperatures involved in the kilning process. Using small amounts of dark grains such as crystal, roasted barley, black patent; and chocolate will contribute greater differences in the taste, aroma, and color of your beer than if only malt extract was used.

Sacks of malted barley, the primary sugar source in all beer, are ready for mashing at a commercial brewery.

Specialty Grains

George Hummel,
Home Sweet Homebrew

What makes brewing with extract and specialty grains different? Imagine you're having guests for dinner and you've decided to make chicken soup. Of course, you're not going to crack open a can of store-bought soup, slop it in a saucepan, heat it up and say, "Here's your dinner!" But maybe you don't have time to take a whole chicken, render it into stock, cook it for several hours, and refrigerate it overnight so you can skim the excess fat. That's a two-day affair. A reasonable compromise would be to take a can of plain chicken stock and add some fresh chicken and vegetables to the pot. Although it wasn't made from scratch, with just a little extra work, you can produce a soup that gives the illusion of having been made from the bird up. The same can be said of beer produced from plain light extract that's been flavored and colored with specialty grains and hops—it tastes much more like it was made from scratch.

Specialty Malt

Introducing specialty grains to your brewing procedure can bring in new nuances of flavors and aromas. You can mix and match the grains; toasted, roasted, and crystallized malts offer a cornucopia of flavor and aroma as well as a palette of colors. Hues from deep burnished gold to dark-as-night

wait for you to explore. Aromatics range from warm biscuits to the deep aromas of dark fruit, dark chocolate, and coffee. All these attributes can be used to make your special brew just a little more enticing and unique.

Extreme Hops

There are countless hop varieties available for brewing. Bitterness varies from subtle to extreme and the aromatics can range from soft floral notes to big, burly, piney aromas. There are the different permutations of all the possible combinations and they are all notes in the symphony of your beer. When you begin to combine these diverse malts and hops along with the huge selection of yeast cultures available to the modern brewer, it becomes obvious that the sky's the limit. Don't be afraid to get out there and brew with all your senses. Smell and chew those grains. Nose those hops. You've got to be a little crazy to be an extreme brewer.

Extreme Malt

Another way to use malt to make an ordinary beer more extreme is to use more of it. The more malt extract used in a batch, the more fermentable sugars you will be left with. The average 5-gallon (19 L) homebrew recipe utilizes about 6 pounds (2.7 kg) of malt extract to create a beer with an average original gravity of 1.050. This will end up producing a beer of around 5 percent alcohol by volume.

(continued)

(continued from page 61)

By adding twice the amount of extract to the same 5-gallon (19-L) batch you will yield a beer of about 10 percent ABV. Because malt sugars are not 100 percent fermentable (they are closer to 70 percent), it's necessary to bump up your hopping rates proportionately. It is generally true that the stronger you make the beer, the sweeter it will be and the more hops you will need to offset that sweetness. Unlike a number of the extreme brewing techniques that will be explored in the coming sections of this chapter, the use of additional or specialty malt should take place during the brewing process as opposed to during fermentation or aging. With this in mind, it's always a good idea to write out a recipe in advance of the brew day so that you will have time to acquire the additional ingredients.

So, why brew with prehopped, colored malt extract or beer kits? Did you get into homebrewing to drink a cookie-cutter beer that the guy down the street made too? Of course not. With all the ingredients that are out there, you'll never have to brew the same beer twice—unless you want to!

> *The earlier hops are added to the boil, the more they will contribute to the taste. The later in the boil they are added, the more they will contribute to the aroma.*

Hops

Brewing beers with more aggressive hopping rates is nothing new. The British first perfected the method back in the late 1700s with their creation of the India Pale Ale style. This was a beer that had a higher alcohol content and a higher hopping level, both of which act as a preservative. The preservative qualities helped the beer last on its long voyage to the British colonies of India, hence the name. The IPA style is probably one of the fastest growing types of craft-brewed and homebrewed beers in the world today. In fact, there is a whole new category that evolved in the U.S. called Imperial or Double IPAs that have more hops and more alcohol than their English counterparts.

Some malt extract cans come prehopped but if you're interested in extreme hopping you will definitely want to add hops above and beyond what's already in the extract. Better still, you can use unhopped malt extract and real pellet or whole-leaf hops to make your beer. As with any kind of cooking, the more pure and natural the ingredients, the more pure and natural the final product will taste.

Hops add bitterness and aroma to beer, but they also act as a natural preservative. Once brewers realized that hops significantly added to a beer's shelf life, they turned their attention away from less successful spicing agents and focused solely on working with hops. When hops are brewed, they release bittering compounds (alpha and beta acids) and aroma compounds (essential oils) that affect the beer differently depending on when they are added to the brewpot.

When brewing beers with pronounced hop character, it's a good idea to extend the boil time from the usual hour to an hour and a half. As the wort boils, the natural resins in the hops that contribute bitterness and aroma melt into an oil and are absorbed into solution. For highly hopped beers, it's important to have a really vigorous boil as the rolling action of the boil will help the hop oils (that tend to pool on the top of the beer) fold themselves into the actual wort. As you brew stronger beers, you'll want to up the hopping rate to compensate for the additional body the beer will have from nonfermentable, excess sugars. Also, higher quality worts tend to absorb less bitterness, so you'll need to add more hops. A good rule of thumb for increasing hop loads for a 5-gallon (19 L) batch is to add 10 percent more boil hops for every ten points of original gravity over 1.060 that the recipe calls for.

There are countless ways to enhance the hop profile of your beers after the wort has been boiled. These methods will contribute aroma and perceived hop bitterness, but won't contribute actual bitterness, as that can only happen during the boil phase. The most common method of postboil hop addition is dry hopping. In this method, pellets or whole leaf hops are added into the carboy once fermentation has slowed down (See page 26, Dry Hopping). You can also add natural hop oil (available at any good homebrew supply source) just before transferring the beer for bottling. As little as 0.04 grams of the oil is all it will take to noticeably increase hop presence in a 5-gallon (19 L)

This tin contains 1½ ounces (32 g) of whole-leaf hops ready to be added to a 5-gallon (19-L) batch of homebrew.

batch of homebrew. Another less common source of late-hopping aroma is to add 1/2 ounce (15 g) of pellets to the heated priming sugar water and stir it into the solution before dumping it into your bottling bucket and transferring the beer on top of it.

Extreme Yeast

Yeast is the organism that eats sugars in order to create alcohol. Using yeast as a component of extreme brewing has been realized in two ways: finding yeast strains that add complexity and distinction to beers of normal alcohol levels, and using yeast strains that are more tolerant of higher alcohol levels to make stronger-than-average beers. There are many yeast strains that have evolved to give flavor and aroma contributions that are now synonymous with the styles of beers they are pitched in. German wheat beer yeasts, for example, give clove and citrus notes to the beer while certain Belgian yeast strains give peppery, spicy notes, and English yeast strains can contribute an estery, fruity profile. All good homebrew ingredient supply sources carry a wide range of yeast strains. There are many more liquid strains (50+) available than dry strains (10+), but dry strains

Because homebrewers often try to make their beers in smaller pots, they end up with less-than-ideal headspace to allow for a vigorous boil. A more vigorous boil of less-dense wort is important because it means better hop utilization and better breakdown of all of the added sugars.

Randall the Enamel Animal

THERE IS A HOPPING technique that we came up with at our brewery called "real-time hopping." This is a method in which you add hop character to the beer at the point that you are actually serving it. However, it only works if the beer is being poured from a tap. We call our hopping invention Randall, the Enamel Animal.

It's an organoleptic hop transducer and there are instructions on how to build you own on our website: www.dogfish.com. Randall is basically a glorified pool filter and we've now built over 300 of these devices for breweries, beer enthusiasts, and homebrewers around the world.

have gained popularity in the past few years due to improved quality and an increase in availability.

When using liquid yeast, it is a good idea to make a starter. A starter is a small batch of beer used to increase the number of yeast cells. This starter batch is then added to a larger volume to help start fermentation quickly. A starter can reduce fermentation start from 24 hours to about 5 hours.

Here are steps for making your own yeast starter:

1. Boil some wort S.G. 1.020–30 using 3–4 tablespoons (45–60 g) malt extract in 2 cups (475 ml) of water for 5 minutes. Increase starter gravity to 1.060 to 1.070 for higher gravity beers.

2. Cool to 75°F (24°C), add yeast and incubate (let sit at that temperature, which is about room temperature) for 12 to 24 hours. (You should see a lot of small bubbles in the wort but little foam on the top.

A collection of exotic sugars used in extreme brewing:

A. Pure cane sugar
B. Demerara sugar
C. Belgian candi sugar, amber
D. Dark brown sugar
E. Belgian candi sugar, light
F. Light brown sugar

Use the starter as soon as possible, ideally within two days. If you're brewing a specific style of beer, it's generally best to seek out the yeast strain traditionally used with that style.

Using different yeast strains or techniques to brew beers of higher-than-average alcohol content is a whole different ballgame. The reason there are no beers or wines that are as strong as distilled sprits like vodka or rum is that, at a certain level, the presence of alcohol is toxic to the yeast; it will erode the walls of the yeast cells and eventually kill the yeast and halt fermentation. However, there are specific yeast strains that are more tolerant to higher alcohol levels and there are certain methods that you can attempt to prolong the life of yeast to ferment beers of higher alcohol levels.

To brew strong beers, you need yeast strains with great attenuation properties. Attenuation is the fancy term for the measurable amount of sugars that yeast can eat. Attenuation is all about the percentage of sugars in a liquid that yeast can convert into alcohol. Brewing yeasts usually attenuate between 65 and 75 percent of the available sugars in the liquid. Again, your supply source will sell yeast strains that are specifically created for fermenting higher-than-average sugar levels. For instance, wine and Champagne yeasts work best on liquids that are targeted to be between 8 and 18 percent alcohol by volume whereas traditional beer yeasts work best on liquids that are targeted to be between 4 and 8 percent alcohol by volume. The problem with using yeast strains that were developed in the wine and Champagne industries is that they tend to dry out beer and give it cidery, vinous qualities. That doesn't mean they don't have a place in homebrewing strong beers. The best way to realize the higher-attenuating properties of wine and Champagne yeast without getting those undesirable notes is to add one of the yeast strains midway through fermentation. The point at which you add that strain, whether Champagne or wine, is determined not by time, but by when your beer has fermented halfway to its projected final gravity. In other words, if you are brewing a strong beer with an original gravity of 1.090 and a projected final gravity of 1.010, then you are hoping to drop 80 points in gravity over the course of the fermentation. To begin fermentation, pitch an ale yeast. Use your hydrometer to determine when the beer has dropped to a gravity of 1.050 (halfway to the projected final gravity of 1.010), then pitch a wine or Champagne yeast to finish the beer down to the final gravity of 1.010. By using an ale yeast for the first half of fermentation, the finished beer will maintain more of the ideal ale taste and aroma characteristics, as opposed to the dry, cidery notes that would have come from pitching a wine or Champagne yeast alone.

A good rule to remember when brewing stronger beers is that they usually like to be pitched with more yeast than beers of normal alcohol content. If you don't pitch enough yeast in a strong beer, you may have a lag time before fermentation takes off. During this lag time your beer is more susceptible to bacteria growth and spoilage. Or you may have an incomplete or stuck fermentation, meaning that the yeast begins to ferment the beer but dies or goes dormant before the targeted final gravity and alcohol content are achieved. In addition to sugar, yeast also likes oxygen (at least during the beginning phase of fermentation). This is why it's a good idea to pour the wort from up high and let it splash as it's transferred from the brewpot to the fermenter. And don't be afraid to vigorously shake the fermenter as it's filling, as that will help more oxygen get into the solution. Many homebrew supply sources sell small aquarium pumps or oxygen tanks with an aeration stone that can be submerged into the wort to add even higher levels of oxygen as the fermentation takes off. Just make sure to stop dosing in oxygen once fermentation begins as the later in the fermentation phase you add oxygen, the more it will contribute cardboard and metallic flavors to the final beer.

You'll run into fewer problems with overpitching than you will with underpitching the yeast when making strong beers. Consider pitching twice the suggested amount of yeast on any beer that has an original gravity of 1.080 or higher. You might also add one package of yeast at the beginning and another package when the fermentation begins to slow down. It's always a good idea to add a bit more sugar (1 cup [200 g] diluted in hot water, then cooled to 80°F [27°C]), if you're adding more yeast late in fermentation to make sure that these new yeast cells have a meal ready for them as they begin their work.

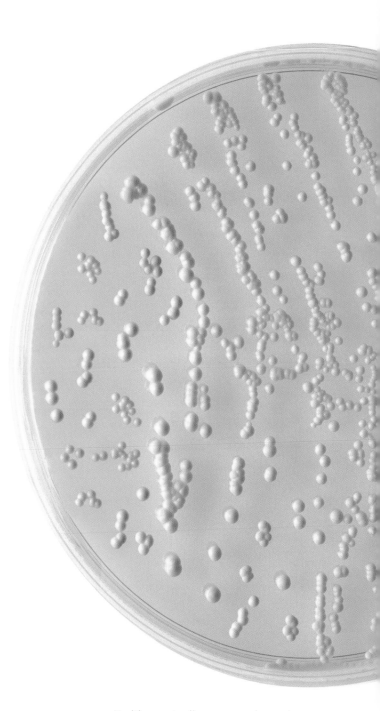

Healthy yeast cells as seen under a microscope

I would suggest using an aquarium pump for the first hour that the wort is in your carboy and then removing it. If the fermentation hasn't taken off by the next day, stick the sanitized pump back in for another hour.

Dry Yeast

When homebrewing first took off in this country during Prohibition, most people made their beers using bread/baker's yeast. The problem with using packaged baker's yeast is that there is a higher presence of wild yeast and bacteria during the drying process. Today, there are a number of companies making a wide range of high-quality dry and liquid brewing yeasts for both the home and commercial brewing communities.

BEYOND THE BASICS

Playing around with the volumes and types of yeast, grains, and hops to add complexity to your beer is only the point where extreme brewing begins. The real departure point, where beer complexity and distinction can be enhanced exponentially, is with the addition of nontraditional ingredients into the brewing process.

Sugar

Augmenting the traditional barley sugars in beer with additional sugar sources is probably the easiest way to add alcohol and complexity to your beer. Before discussing what kinds of sugars work best in the brewing process, it will help to better understand how all sugars work during fermentation.

Sugars are basic carbohydrates that can either be simple (monosaccharide) or linked together to form complex starches or sugars. Starches, like those found in barley, have to be broken down into simpler forms (through malting and mashing) before they can be eaten by the yeast.

While sugar will add alcohol and complexity to beer, be careful how much you add, as too much sugar will contribute a ciderlike dryness to your beer. A good rule of thumb is to never make a beer that has more than 20 percent of its sugar base come from adjunct sugars or less than 80 percent malt sugars.

Sugars can be added during the boil or during fermentation. The later in the process they are added, the more aroma and flavor they will add to your beer. If you are brewing a really strong beer (10 percent alcohol by volume or higher with an original gravity of 1.090 or higher), add the sugars during fermentation. If the beer has a gravity that's too high (too much sugar) before you begin fermentation, the yeast might be overwhelmed and not ferment the beer properly. If you are adding sugars during fermentation, sterilize them in hot water and then let the diluted solution cool to less than 80°F (27°C) before adding it to the beer. Remember to leave room in the carboy for sugar additions if you intend to make them. As previously recommended, use a 6-gallon (23-L) carboy for 5-gallon (19-L) batches of beer that are made with sugar additions during fermentation. The more sugars you add, the more the yeast will grow and the less space there will be in the carboy. This will increase the risk of both beer and yeast bubbling out the top of the airlock and down the sides of the carboy, which would be both messy and unsanitary.

As an extreme homebrewer, you have an almost limitless variety of sugar sources to explore. This exploration has been one of my favorite tasks at Dogfish Head. We have made beers with molasses, beet sugar, cane sugar, all kinds of brown sugar, maple syrup, and honey. Most sugars have a slightly different percentage of fermentability; cane sugar, for instance, is more highly fermentable than molasses. A very loose rule of thumb for adding sugars is that 1 pound (455 g) will add roughly ten points to the original gravity of the beer. If you are adding them during fermentation, remember to record those bumps in gravity for the recipe—even though they won't be added until after the brew day.

Fruits

Brewing with fruit has been a tradition in Belgium for centuries and has become a regular activity in the craft brewing scene as well. There is a great difference between varieties of fruit as to how much flavor, aroma, and sugars they contribute to a brew. The first decision facing the extreme brewer who wants to incorporate fruit into a batch of beer is which variety to add. The second decision is what format this fruit will be used in: whole fresh fruit, puréed frozen fruit, natural fruit extract, or artificial fruit extract. Unless you are a giant commercial brewer trying to save pennies, there is never an excuse for using artificial fruit flavors; they taste and smell artificial because they *are* artificial. One of the points of homebrewing is to make something special that is a reflection of your personality. You don't want to be known as the artificial beer guy (or gal).

EXTREME FRUITS

Extreme fruit quantities for a 5-gallon (19-L) batch successfully used at Dogfish Head follow. Remember that a bigger brewpot and carboy may be needed to accommodate additional fruit volumes. In this section, the recommended volume and suggested usage point during the brew are for recipes utilizing fresh (or dried) fruits. If you'd prefer to use puréed fruit, recalibrate your recipes by halving the volume of fruit and adding the purée after the boil is over but before transfer-ring to fermentation. Let the puréed fruit steep in the hot wort for at least 20 minutes and then transfer it into the carboy along with the beer before pitching the yeast. Some varieties of whole fruits, such as apples and pears, are more difficult to break down during fermentation and the solids can trap both yeast and flavor components, affecting the utilization rates.

FRUIT	QUANTITY	TIME	TIP
Apricots, chopped and dried	4 pounds (1.8 kg)	10 minutes before the end of a 60-minute boil.	Allow fruit to be transferred into carboy for fermentation.
Arctic Cloudberries	6 pounds (2.7 kg)	End of 60-minute boil.	Try to maintain a wort temperature between 160°F and 170°F (71°C–77°C) for at least 20 minutes before cooling your wort. Strain fruit solids before transferring cooled wort to the carboy. This timing method will pasteurize the fruit without boiling it, which would set the natural pectin and cast a haze in the finished beer.
Black Currants	8 pounds (3.6 kg)	End of 60-minute boil.	Try to maintain a wort temperature between 160°F and 170°F (71°C–77°C) for at least 20 minutes before cooling the wort. Strain fruit solids before transferring cooled wort to the carboy.
Blueberries, crushed	10 pounds (4.5 kg)	End of 60-minute boil.	Try to maintain a wort temperature between 160°F and 170°F (71°C–77°C) for at least 20 minutes before cooling the wort. Strain fruit solids before transferring cooled wort to the carboy.
White Muscat Grape Concentrate	16 ounces (475 ml)	After fermentation.	Best added after fermentation takes off in the carboy. (Be sure to leave ample head space for yeast growth.)
Raisins	6 ounces (125 g)	10 minutes before the end of a 60-minute boil.	Allow fruit to be transferred into carboy for fermentation.
Raspberries, fresh	8 pounds (3.6 kg)	End of 60-minute boil.	Try to maintain a wort temperature between 160°F and 170°F (71°C–77°C) for at least 20 minutes before cooling the wort. Strain fruit solids before transferring cooled wort to the carboy.
Sour Cherries, crushed	10 pounds (4.5 kg)	End of 60-minute boil.	Try to maintain a wort temperature between 160°F and 170°F (71°C–77°C) for at least 20 minutes before cooling the wort. Allow cherry solids, pits and all, to be transferred to the carboy for fermentation.
Strawberries, fresh and quartered	10 pounds (4.5 kg)	End of 60-minute boil.	Try to maintain a wort temperature between 160°F and 170°F (71.1°C–77°C) for at least 20 minutes before cooling the wort. Strain fruit solids before transferring cooled wort to the carboy.
Sweet Cherries, crushed	8 pounds (3.6 kg)	End of 60-minute boil.	Try to maintain a wort temperature between 160°F and 170°F (71°C–77°C) for at least 20 minutes before cooling the wort. Strain fruit solids before transferring cooled wort to the carboy.

As a general rule, tart fruits tend to add more aroma (sour cherries, orange rind) and sweet fruits tend to add more flavor (raspberries, blueberries). Start with a beer recipe that's relatively light in alcohol, hops, and color. Dark grains and high hopping rates will only reduce the presence of fruit aromas and flavors. That's not to say it can't be done; at Dogfish Head we have played around with fruits like apricots and highly hopped beers that feature pungent West Coast hop varieties like Cascade and Columbus. But in general, you don't want the desired fruit flavors competing with other heightened flavors in your beer.

At our brewery, we use either whole fresh fruit or aseptic frozen fruit purées. As with most flavoring agents (i.e., hops and sugars), fruit can be added during the boil or during fermentation. If you intend to use fresh fruit, the time to add it is toward the end of the boil. If it's added too early in the boil, many of the flavors and aromas of the fruit will be released into the air with the steam. By adding it late in the boil, you capture more of the flavor and aroma and you also sterilize the fruit. This is critical since fresh fruit invariably has some small amount of bacteria or wild yeast present on its surface. If you wish to add fresh fruit during fermentation, for sterilizing reasons steep it in 180°F-plus (82.2°C) water for at least 30 minutes and let it come back down below 70°F (21.1°C) before adding it to the carboy. The later the fruit is added during fermentation, the more flavor and aroma it will contribute. Adding fruit postfermentation is not recommended as you want the yeast to eat the sugars from the fruit while the beer is still in the carboy. Remember, if there are available sugars in this extract post fermentation they can cause overcarbonation in the bottle. However, you can find some natural flavor concentrates that are devoid of sugars and they can be added post fermentation to enhance the fruit aroma of the beer, but my experience leads me to believe they won't contribute much in the terms of natural flavor.

At Dogfish Head, we have had great success using aseptic puréed fruit as well. Because it's in a sterile package it doesn't need to be heated up to use it. Even frozen strawberries and raspberries from the grocery store work great in homebrewing. Just make sure they're not packed with additives and preservatives that might immobilize the yeast. You can add them to your beer at the end of the boil and they will serve two functions: They will add the desired fruit flavor

HISTORICAL NOTE

Sugar Sources

Traditionally, a brewer's sugar sources (in addition to malt) depended on the geographic region. British brewers made beers fortified with cane sugar or molasses that came from their colonies in the Caribbean or Africa. In northeast Europe, where beets were prevalent, brewers would use beet sugars in their beers. In Colonial America, pumpkin and corn were readily available for brewing. With the modernization of transportation and packaging techniques, almost all types of sugars are available now to brewers worldwide. These days, it's the personal preference of the brewer and not geographic considerations that determine which sugars go into the beer.

Yeast and Assorted Fermentation Cultures

David Logsdon, Wyeast Founder

Two aspects of extreme brewing, the high gravity style and regimens that use multiple strains, (including bacteria and wild type yeasts) have specific and unique requirements that must be considered and prepared for well in advance of brew day.

High-gravity wort is hell on yeast. The osmotic pressure of high sugar levels can make metabolism of the available nutrients by yeast difficult, which is why starting with healthy yeast is of paramount importance. After enduring the initial stress of high sugar levels, alcohol toxicity sets in as the specific gravity of the wort drops, resulting in a great deal of stress for the yeast at both ends of fermentation. Another option is to start with a wort of moderate specific gravity and use meter-concentrated sugars in the fermenter, which will keep the overall gravity below 1.080, reducing the risk of osmotic shock. Choose highly attenuated ale, wheat, wine, and Belgian strains of yeast for best ethanol tolerance.

High-gravity beers need pitch rates that are about three to five times higher than typical beers.

Oxygen requirements increase accordingly with a higher pitch rate. Oxygen doesn't dissolve well in high-gravity worts, so it's best to add pure oxygen (preferably not air) frequently for the first fourteen hours after the yeast is pitched. Adding yeast nutrients, such as zinc or other minerals and various coenzymes, will help maximize yeast metabolism. Keeping the fermentation process warm, with occasional agitation, will improve the end result.

There is nothing like the complexity of a Flanders or lambic style beer that can be attained using multiple yeast strains. These types of beers really improve by making a dextrin (simple starch) wort to feed to the lactic acid bacteria (typically used to ferment and culture) and *Brettanomyces* yeast. Add all yeast and bacterial cultures at the onset of fermentation. The different strains will kick in as conditions develop as long as the wort contains adequate complex sugars. Give them all time to grow: you will be glad you did. And while you're at it, why go small? These beers (and the cultures) work well beyond 9 percent alcohol by volume.

and aromas, and they will also help to cool the beer down to yeast pitching temperature, more quickly. If adding frozen fruit during fermentation, let it thaw in a clean pot before adding it as it will bring down the beer's temperature and possibly stall or even halt yeast activity. Remember to leave enough head space in your fermenter to add the fruit and contain the subsequent yeast growth that will come with the additional fruit sugars. The presence of fermentable sugars in different varieties of fruit is much broader than in different sugar sources. For this reason, there is no broad rule of thumb on how much fruit to add for a 5-gallon (19-L) batch.

Herbs and Spices

Herbs and spices will give you the most bang for your buck when making an exotic beer as only small amounts of them are needed in order to affect the flavor and aroma of the final beer.

As with fruit beers, the later herbs and spices are added, the more flavor and aroma they will contribute. At Dogfish Head, we have had more success adding spices and herbs at the end of the boil as opposed to during or after fermentation. It seems that many herbs and spices won't relinquish their goodness unless they are steeped like tea at higher temperatures. Avoid adding any oily spices such as anise and licorice root late in fermentation, as the natural oils can prevent heat retention, making the final beer appear to be flat and undercarbonated. Spices and herbs added during or after fermentation should be doubled in quantity, as a lot of the flavor and aroma will be absorbed by the yeast that will settle to the bottom of the carboy before transferring for bottling. At our brewery, we've also had good results adding half the quantity of an herb or spice called for in a recipe to the boil and the other half after fermentation.

Many herbs and spices can be purchased from any homebrew supply source, but I prefer to buy mine at health food stores or from natural ingredient supply companies to assure quality and freshness. It's also fun to browse through stores and catalogs that have a great selection of herbs and spices, as you might stumble upon a new ingredient idea for an extreme beer. This is how roasted chicory ended up being an integral ingredient in one of our popular stouts.

HISTORICAL NOTE

Historical Brew

Long before focusing on hops, brewers were experimenting with different herbs and spices. In fact, hops weren't the dominant spicing agent in beer until the fifteenth century. Spruce tips, cinnamon, vanilla beans, grains of paradise, nutmeg, allspice and juniper are but a few of the spices that were even more popular then than they are in extreme brews today.

Rosemary

Juniper berries

Lemongrass

St. John's Wort

Star anise

Tarragon

Chives

Hawthorne fruit powder

Oregano

Dill weed

Green peppercorns

Laurel leaves

Lavender

To deepen the complexity of your extreme beer, add herbs and spices to complement the other flavors.

WOOD-AGING BEER

When beer is fermented or stored in wood for prolonged periods of time, it undergoes subtle physical changes. Natural tannins and lignins (phenolic compounds) within the wood are released into the beer. These factors contribute the earthy, soft, vanilla, notes that come with aging beer in wood. For the purpose of exploring the world of extreme brewing, this discussion will focus on techniques for using wood to add complexity of aroma and flavor to your beer.

Wood is most commonly used in brewing during a late phase of fermentation or after fermentation during a prolonged aging phase. Many of today's great Belgian breweries are famous for fermenting and aging their beers in wood casks or giant oak tanks. As a home-brewer, you can either ferment the beer in actual wood barrels or add wood chips to the glass carboy before fermentation. As for which beer styles work best for aging on wood, that's up to you. In general, stronger beers (8 percent alcohol by volume or above) are recommended, as their higher alcohol levels will strip more of the aroma and flavor from the wood. Stronger beers are more durable and will often improve with extended aging times.

EXTREME HERBS AND SPICES

Herbs and spices that we have used successfully at Dogfish Head and their recommended quantities follow. As with all suggestions in this book, these are exactly that, suggestions. Don't be afraid to let your freak-flag fly and experiment with more, less, or even different ingredients than the ones listed here. Use a specialty grain sack for herbs and spices so after flavors are extracted, solids can be easily removed before fermentation. Each one shows the recommended amount for a 5-gallon (19 L) batch and the best point in the brewing process to add it:

HERB	QUANTITY	TIME
Allspice	0.5 ounce (15 g)	50 minutes into a 60-minute boil.
Anise	0.5 ounce (15 g)	40 minutes into a 60-minute boil.
Cardamom seed	1 ounce (28 g)	50 minutes into a 60-minute boil.
Chicory, crushed	3 ounces (85 g)	Added with specialty grains in a sack.
Coriander	1 1/2 ounces (43 g)	50 minutes into a 60-minute boil.
Cinnamon sticks	2 sticks	50 minutes into a 60-minute boil.
Coffee, dark roast	16 ounces (455 g)	End of the boil.
Ginger, fresh chopped	2 ounces (24 g)	50 minutes into a 60-minute boil.
Grains of paradise	0.2 ounces (6 g)	50 minutes into a 60-minute boil.
Juniper berries, crushed	2 ounces (55 g)	50 minutes into a 60-minute boil.
Licorice root	1 1/2 ounces (43 g)	40 minutes into a 60-minute boil.
Rosemary	1 1/2 ounces (43 g)	50 minutes into a 60-minute boil.
Saffron threads	10 threads	50 minutes into a 60-minute boil.
Spruce tips	2 ounces (55 g)	50 minutes into a 60-minute boil.
St. John's Wort	2 ounces (55 g)	50 minutes into a 60-minute boil.
Valerian	1 ounce (28 g)	40 minutes into a 60-minute boil.

The later in the process that fruits, herbs, or spices are added, the more they will contribute to the taste and aroma of the final beer.

BARREL-AGING BEER

If you decide to use a barrel for aging, there are still some other decisions you'll need to make. First, you'll have to decide whether you want to use French or American oak. American is more pungent while French oak is subtler. The next decision is new oak versus used. New oak will change the flavor, aroma, and color of the beer much more rapidly than used oak. If you intend to go with used oak, the next decision to make is if it's oak from the wine, brandy, port, or whiskey industries. Whatever alcohol was last used in the barrel is sure to influence the profile of the beer that will age in it. Remember that wood is porous, so a small amount of beer and alcohol will evaporate through the walls of the barrel. In order to prevent the beer from oxidizing while it's aging, top off the barrel occasionally with more beer to keep it full. Bourbon casks are also useful for aging beer and enhancing complexity.

Rows of barreled wood-aged beer are actively fermenting.

WOOD CHIPS

Barrel aging can be fun but it is time consuming and requires a fair amount of dedication. This is why it's easier to start playing around with wood by using chips instead of barrels. Using chips will eliminate the need for additional expensive brewing equipment purchases. As most barrels are large (55 gallons [208 L]), it would take many, many 5-gallon (19-L) batches to fill one. To use chips, all that's needed is a second carboy. Simply transfer the beer from the carboy you fermented into a second sterilized carboy, add the chips (sterilize chips in an oven at 300°F [150°C] for 30 minutes), and replace the stopper and airlock on the top of the carboy. If you don't want to spend the extra money on a second carboy, add the sterilized wood chips just after fermentation begins. The presence of chips will actually assist in the fermentation process (more surface area for the yeast) and also help to clarify the beer as the yeast settles toward the end of fermentation.

So, how much wood should be added for a 5-gallon (19-L) batch? There is no easy answer here. The wide range would probably be from 2 to 4 ounces (55 to 115 g) of wood chips per batch assuming that the chips are thin and numerous. One giant 4-ounce (115-g) chunk of wood will impart substantially less wood character than many small chips that add up to 4 ounces (115 g), as they create more surface area for the beer to be in contact with. New oak chips will contribute aroma and flavor to the beer in less than two weeks while used oak chips will take much longer, depending mainly on how many times they've already been used. Taste and smell samples of your beer periodically, and be ready to transfer it for bottling once the desired wood character is present. While oak is the most common wood, there are brewers out there using birch, cherry, and beech wood as well.

A batch of homebrew gains depth of flavor from the addition of French oak chips.

Wood Barrels

WOOD has been used to house and transport fermented beverages for nearly as long as man has been making them. Although the first brewers in China, Greece, and Egypt used different versions of ceramic vessels to house and transport their beverages, ultimately, wood was cheaper, more durable, and easier to construct. By the first century CE it had replaced ceramics as the vessel of choice. Today, there are a handful of tradition-minded breweries in Belgium, England, and the United States that utilize wood in the brewing and aging of beer. In fact, one of the biggest breweries in the world uses strips of beech wood during fermentation—not for aroma or flavor but to aid in yeast growth and settling.

A close-up of yeast escaping an actively fermenting barrel

Wild Yeast and Bacteria

Up until now, the importance of sanitation in brewing has been adamantly emphasized. Without proper sanitation during fermentation, bacteria and wild yeast can grow and overcome the yeast that's been pitched. Yet there are styles of beer that have been brewed for centuries that intentionally incorporate wild yeast and certain types of bacteria into the brewing process. With great care and a little skill, you can easily attempt brewing variations of these extreme beers at home.

"Extreme brewing is the creation of a beer that falls outside the normal parameters of a beer style. Take an IPA and add twice as many hops, and that's extreme. Take a regular stout and add twice as much original gravity to create twice as much alcohol, and that's extreme. Take a regular Belgian-style ale and add Brett to it for sourness and the "horsey" effect, and that's extreme. Take any beer and age it in an oak barrel, wait a year, and you'll have an extreme beer."

Adam Avery,
Avery Brewing Company

CHAPTER 5

Understanding and Enjoying Extreme Beer

WHILE HOMEBREWING IS a rewarding hobby in and of itself, let's face it, for many of us it is a means to an end: enjoying great home-made beer. Becoming proficient in any hobby takes practice, and the same holds true for both brewing and tasting beer. Although the recipes in this book are mostly for beers that fall outside of normal beer style parameters, it's important to have an understanding of how traditional beer styles are made. In this chapter, you'll find a general summary of some of the more common beer styles as well as some useful techniques for how best to hold a beer tasting (whether solo or in a group) using your senses. In the same way that you must be comfortable with the equipment needed to make beer, you must also be comfortable with the equipment needed to enjoy and analyze beer: your body and mind. Truly enjoying beer is an artform that requires all five senses.

A collection of American craft-brewed beers with diverse of packaging and labels

AN OVERVIEW OF BEER STYLES

American craft brewers, Belgian brewers, and home-brewers have been instrumental in expanding the definition of what beer can be. However, it is helpful to get a handle on some of the more popular, traditional styles of beer that are enjoyed through out the world before we set off to explore new possibilities. This is only a partial list of traditional beer styles, but over 95 percent of the beer being produced and enjoyed through the modern world is a variation on one of the following styles.

At one point, long ago, all beers were ales. Using a top-fermenting yeast, ale brewers were able to brew a wide range of styles. Even today, in the countries with the most vibrant craft beer communities—(the U.S., Belgium, the U.K., Germany, and Italy)—many of the small breweries focus heavily on full-bodied, bold ales. However, these efforts don't reflect predominant modern tastes, and they haven't for a long time. Through trial and error, brewers learned that certain yeast strains could ferment beers at lower-than-normal temperature. While these cooler fermentations took a longer period to complete, they led to beers that were more crisp and clearer than ales. Once commercial refrigeration became the norm during the industrial revolution, brewers could better control fermentation temperatures. German, Austrian, and Czechoslovakian breweries began commercial production of lagers at around the same time. Also during this time, glassware was replacing earthenware as the packaging of choice and the light, clear lager styles appeared more impressive and brighter than the darker, murkier ales when packaged in a newfangled bottle.

Continental Pilsner

Pilsner is by far the most popular style of beer the world over, but a pilsner beer means different things to different cultures. These beers are brewed using 100 percent malted barley as a fermented sugar source. They are relatively dry and hoppy with a light strawlike color and a nice, foamy white head. These beers usually lager, or age, for long periods of time, which contributes bready, yeast character while also bringing great clarity to the beer. Spicy Saaz and Hallertau are the most common hops used in this style of beer. Pilsners should be served cold (50°F [10°C]) from a tall, fluted, straight-sided glass.

American Pilsner

Since the end of Prohibition in the United States, the pilsner style has gotten lighter and lighter. The core and light brands of America's biggest producers (Anheuser-Busch, Molson-Coors, and SAB-Miller) are each sold as pilsner styles although they have little in common with their continental counterparts. The hop level in the American varieties is much lower than that of their Old-World brethren. The most critical difference comes from the fermentable sugar source— all three of America's biggest breweries cut their grain bill by replacing a fraction of the malt in their beers' recipes with either rice or corn. This makes for a beer that is extremely light in color, taste, and aroma. These beers are brewed to be drunk ice cold from the can, bottle, or straight-sided pint glass.

Bock

A strong Bavarian lager, bock (meaning billy goat) beers are headstrong and have a kick like a that of a billy goat. There are Dutch, Danish, and Austrian versions of this style as well. Bocks are amber–to–dark red in color and usually between 6 and 9 percent alcohol by volume. Eisbocks are an interesting substyle made by allowing the beer to partially freeze; this separates the stronger beer from the ice, resulting in a beer that is stronger still. Bock beers are best enjoyed cool (about 55°F [13°C]) from a stein or beer mug.

Good News

THERE ARE LOTS more beer styles than those outlined here. To learn about them in more detail, check out: craftbeer.com, style finder section to find a world of beer.

Dortmunder

These pale beers, sometimes called "export" or "special," are a little maltier and sweeter than a pilsner and a bit stronger in alcohol as well. Dortmunders are best served in a stemmed tulip goblet at cool (55°F [13°C]) temperatures.

Munich or Helles

Munich, or Helles, beers are less hoppy, and more malty than most variations of a pilsner. The hopping profile is most noticeable in the bitterness of the beer and not as much in the aroma. Traditionally, these beers are served in giant, 1-liter steins so it's a good thing that they tend to have lower alcohol contents. They are best served cold (50°F [10°C]).

Pale Ale

This traditional English style is not at all pale in comparison to the light commercial lagers being brewed across the world today, but it was a very pale beer in comparison to the other ale styles popular centuries ago. Before the pale ale gained favor in Britain, browns, porters, and stouts ruled the roost. A pale ale was at first a stronger version of a bitter style beer. Both of these styles tend to be aggressively hopped with a fruity, spicy aroma that comes from both the ale yeast and the hops. Serve cool (55°F [13°C]) from a traditional straight-sided pint glass.

India Pale Ale

This might be the first extreme beer style to gain international favor. Originally, it was brewed in the United Kingdom to last on the long journey from the mainland to the colony in India. Both the high-hopping and high-alcohol levels make this beer sturdy and aggressive. It is best served from a traditional, straight-sided pint glass at 55°F (13°C).

Brown Ale

These beers are probably the offspring of the earliest beer styles. As with pale ales and bitters, brown ales have a U.K. draft counterpart known as "mild." Both milds and brown ales tend to be maltier than either pale ales or IPAs. Brown ales usually have more subtle carbonation than their pale counterparts and modern versions are typically brewed with some proportion of darker crystal or chocolate malted barley for color and body. Serve at 55°F (13°C) from a beer mug or straight-sided pint.

Stout and Porter

The stout and porter styles are almost kissing cousins. Brewed since the early 1700s, the porter style is really the predecessor to stout. Porters are very dark but not quite opaque like a stout. Held up to the light, a light ruby red hue should subtly shine through. Porter is usually brewed with a bit of black patent malt but isn't as bitter or roasty as stout, which get its roasty character from a high proportion of roasted barley. Stouts and porters are best served cool, but not cold, at 55°F (13°C) from a pint glass or a tulip stem glass.

Strong Ales

This umbrella category could include everything from barley wines to malt liquors, Belgian tripels and dubbels. These warming beers of higher alcohol levels stand in defiance to the light lagers that dominate the commercial beer landscape. There is no one style of strong ale, but a few generalizations about these beers can be safely made. The stronger the beer is, the more profound the flavors. Alcohol acts as a phantom ingredient and intensifies the flavors of a beer on the palate. Strong beers tend to improve with age and are excellent candidates for cellaring and multiyear vintage tastings. They are best drunk at cellar temperatures (55°F–60°F [13°–17°C]) from a snifter or a red wine glass.

"The brewers we met and conversed with on our trip to Belgium live, breathe, and die by this notion of extreme brewing, and for that, I celebrate and revel in their uniqueness and eccentric beers and behaviors."

Tomme Arthur,
Port Brewing Company

"While every brewer has the opportunity to become an extreme brewer, not every brewer understands the goals and ambitions of those who embrace the wild child inside that we have come to recognize as extreme brewing. To me, the essence of an extreme brewer is someone who is committed to myriad flavors in their beers *and* who embraces whichever means—traditional, unconventional, or innovation—as a way of reaching a specific flavor-driven goal."

Tomme Arthur,
Port Brewing Company

working knowledge of the smell of hops and the taste of sweet, unfermented wort. What remains is to fine-tune the senses so that all of them are able to truly appreciate the experience of tasting and ingesting the all-natural brews you have so carefully crafted.

1. **Sound** This is probably the most straightforward and basic sense used in the perception of beer, but for the homebrewer it's critical. If you are like me, you are always anxious to try a batch of beer that you have recently bottled. You know you should wait a few weeks after bottling to allow the beer to carbonate in the bottle, but you'll probably be tempted to open a bottle after five or six days. A watched case never carbonates. When you put the bottle, opener to the cap and bring it close to year ear you are hoping to hear that magical "FFFFT!"—the sound of a well-carbonated bottle of beer being opened. Beyond carbonation, there actually isn't much to be gained in listening to your beer. Still, carbonation is critical and the sound of a carboy bubbling during fermentation and a bottle being opened are like music to a homebrewer's ears.

2. **Sight** In beer appreciation, you'll first use vision to examine the bottle you're about to open. Inspect it to see that the bottle is clean, that there isn't a line of sediment in the neck, that the cap isn't rusted, and that not much sediment has settled to the bottom. As you pour the beer into a glass, pay attention to the head retention (does it keep a head or does it immediately dissipate?), the clarity, and the color of the beer. Some beer styles, like wheat beers, are supposed to be hazy and unfiltered, but sometimes, a haze can form on a beer that is spoiled. Color is critical too, especially if you are drinking a beer that purports to be of a certain style. Remember that the color of the beer is going to be affected by the quantity of light in the room where you are. Holding the beer up to eye level between you and the room's greatest light source is the best way to most completely consider the color of the beer. Beer will seem to be lighter when judged against a dark background, and it will appear to be darker when judged against a light background.

3. **Touch** Of course, you aren't going to dip your fingers into the beer—the oils on your skin will adversely affect the beer's head retention. (And you won't get much pleasure from the experience anyway.) When touch is mentioned in context with beer it's actually referencing the mouth, specifically the lips and tongue. Through touch you gauge both the temperature and the texture (mouth-feel/viscosity) of the beer. The brain knows that if you taste something ice cold, you won't experience as much flavor from that substance. That's because taste buds are essentially para-lyzed and incapable of performing their job if the substance is too cold. Also, remember that the body's temperature is around 99°F (37°C) and the beer you are putting in it is around 50°F (10°C). As the beer warms in the mouth, it causes the carbon dioxide to create that pleasant tickle you get with a good sip of beer. Touch is a matter of pressure on the nerve cells; thus, beer lovers are in luck because the tongue and lips are among the most sensitive parts of our bodies. Fuller-bodied beers produce more pressure on the nerve endings in the mouth. That is why barley wine is perceived as thick and chewy, and a wit beer as light and efferves-cent. There is no point in swishing a beer around in your mouth for more than a few seconds as the mouth quickly adapts to the touch of the substance. You are better off swallowing the first sip, waiting a few seconds, then taking a second sip of the beer to consider for an additional few seconds. As you take a sip, don't suck the beer into your throat, let it wash around your teeth and tongue as naturally as possible.

4. **Smell** The process of smelling something is actually much more complicated than one might initially think. People often assume that they taste the nuances of what they eat and drink when in fact, they smell them. The sense of smell detects information about the chemical makeup of the beer and alerts you to dif-ferent levels of additives or possible contaminants. Something else that's amazing about the sense of smell is how strongly it is tied to memory. We are always subconsciously comparing the taste of something against our memory bank of tastes we have

already experienced. Just smelling a well-hopped IPA makes my mouth water, whereas the smell of cheap whiskey can make me dry heave in response to a memory of sneaking into my parents' liquor cabinet as a teenager. So beer that reminds you of a great beer experience you've already had will most like rate higher in your perception than one that is unlike any beer you have tried before. That doesn't mean this new beer won't grow on you—it's just that we are all guilty of forming immediate first impressions: even our reflexive smell perception is implicated in this guilt. Our smelling system basically detects molecular chemical components that are dispersed in the air. We sniff these molecules into the nasal passage (which rubs up against the memory section of our brains). Sniffing more vigorously doesn't really add up to smelling anything more intensely, as doing so will just force more of the molecules into our lungs instead of allowing them to linger in our nasal passage. So, when you hold your nose above a glass of beer, take a series of short sniffs as you are tipping it back for your first taste to fully appreciate the olfactory effects of the beer. Any blockage to the nasal area—whether it be second-hand smoke or congestion from a cold—will severely retard your ability to gauge the smell of your beer, so make sure you are doing your beer tasting in a clean, well-ventilated area. Also remember that your sense of smell, like that of touch, acclimates fairly quickly. This phenomenon is obvious when you begin to pump gas into your car. Initially, all you can smell is gas but by the time the tank if full, you are so acclimated that you barely smell the gas at all.

5. Taste The final sensory frontier. But remember that taste and flavor are not interchangeable terms. Taste is a component of flavor but so are touch and smell. Like smell, the tasting process is related to the ingestion of the natural chemical components in the beer. There are four sections to the tongue that detect different types of taste. This is why it's necessary to slowly swish a beer around in the mouth for a couple of seconds before fully appreciating all of the taste components of this beer. Sweetness is detected on the front tip of the tongue, saltiness on the next quarter, sourness on the sides, and bitterness is picked up in the back. Although wine judges taste and spit, you couldn't properly judge a beer without swallowing it because bitterness is such a key component to beer (unlike wine) and you cannot fully experience the bitterness on the back of your tongue unless you swallow what you're tasting. It's important to stay away from spicy or acidic foods as they will stun the taste buds and alter taste perceptions while you are evaluating a beer. At our brewery, we keep boxes of innocuous oyster cracker on hand to chomp on between beer samples as a way of clearing our palates.

Flavor is subjective. If you are like me, your first tastes of lambics or IPAs were not immediately pleasant, as they represented a great departure from what your palate and brain accepted as "beer" back then. If you are holding a tasting in which a number of people are participating, odds are that some are going to be more acclimated to beer flavors than others. The goal is to expand horizons and share information and impressions, not to stump or bully the other tasters into agreeing with your own perceptions. It's helpful to keep a beer journal with tasting notes of all the different beers that you come across. There are even beer judging guidelines (available at most homebrew supply stores) that walk you though a very analytical point system on which to judge beers. As a brewer or hardcore beer enthusiast, you will probably soon notice that evaluating the beer you're drinking has become a reflexive action. I can't try a beer without subconsciously evaluating it and for that, I'm glad. I'm always looking to create pleasant, new experiences to stuff into my beer memory bank.

> "In present-day craft brewing, extreme brewing means fermenting higher alcohol beers, adding more hops, using barrels, or using wild yeast and bacteria. But, really, it's the small breweries that were courageous enough twenty-five years ago to make a hoppy beer or a barley wine. This was the true beginning of extreme brewing."
>
> Vinnie Cilurzo,
> Russian River Brewing Company

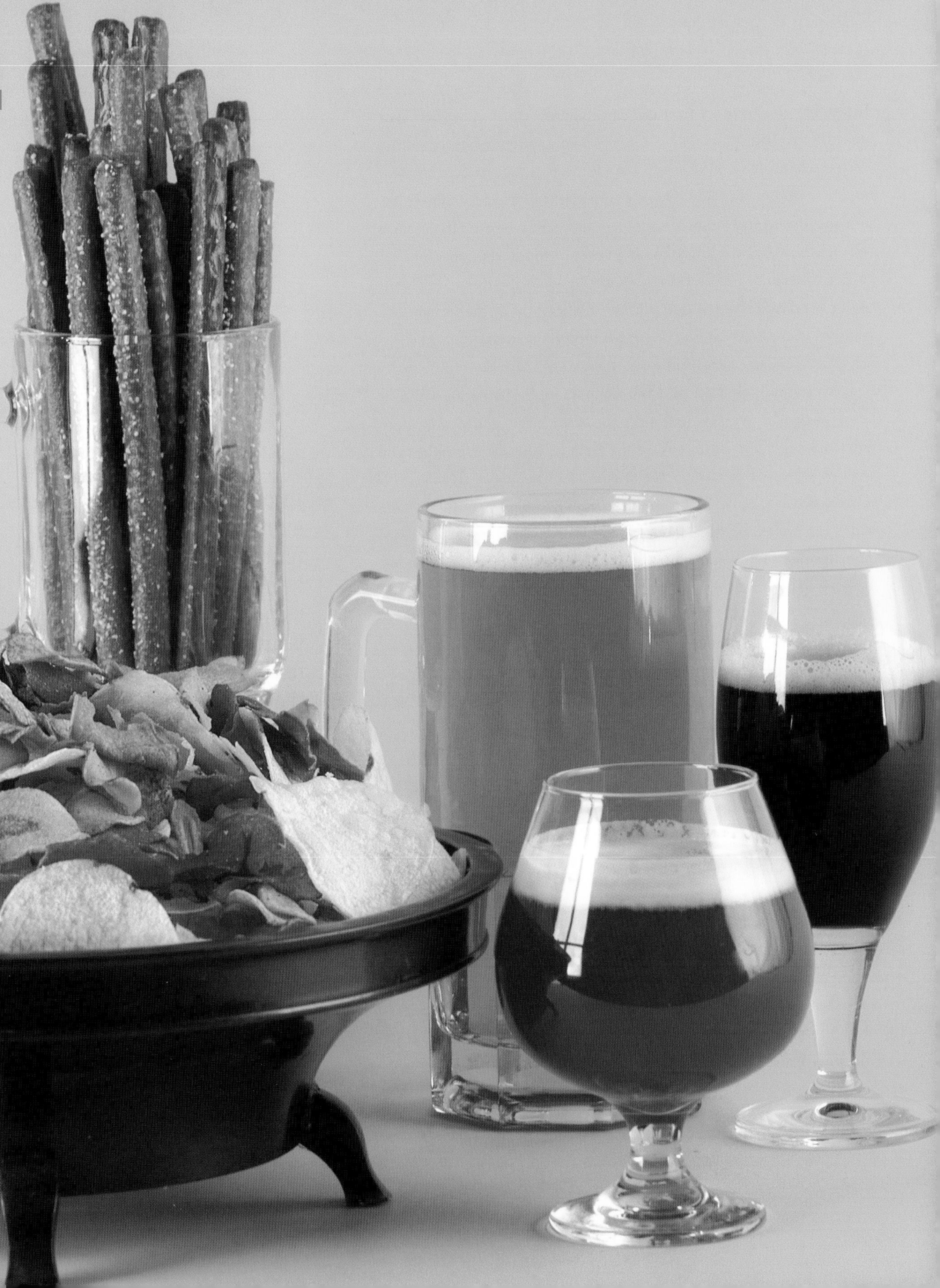

PART 2

Extreme Brewing
at Home

AS I THINK BACK to the first few batches of homebrew that I made over a decade ago, I am amazed that the beer was drinkable at all. Knowing what I know now about the importance of organization, sanitation, and following a recipe, I realize that the brewing process could have been much smoother if I had paid attention to those details. That said, it couldn't have been any more fun. I remember my friend and I sipping on bottles of store-bought beer as our first batch came to a boil and feeling the same sense of exhilaration you feel as you click to the top of a rollercoaster. HOLD ON TIGHT, HERE WE GO! I used to think that recipes were for sissies and that winging it was the jazz equivalent of brewing—the only way to go. The truth is, just because you are making an extreme beer or a beer with nontraditional ingredients, doesn't mean the process won't benefit from a well thought out recipe. Chapters six through eleven provide recipes for making hand-crafted beers at home, including ten recipes from world-renowned master brewers. Chapter ten shows you how to enjoy the fruits of your labor with advice on beer pairing and a bounty of recipes for all kinds of foods, from steak to ice cream, that use beer as an ingredient. Who knows, you may even turn someone else on to the joys of homebrewing.

CHAPTER 6

Extreme Ales

I WOULD BET THAT ninety percent of the beers being homebrewed today are ales. Ale yeasts work at more easily maintained temperatures (around 70°F [21°C]) than lager yeasts, which require cooler fermenting temperatures. Ales also tend to be ready to drink in about half the time as a traditional lager. For these reasons, most small, commercial, craft breweries tend to focus on producing ales. At Dogfish Head, we never even attempted to brew a lager until five years into our existence and we didn't bottle a lager (our imperial pilsner) until almost eleven years after we opened. As the recipes included in this chapter will show, there are huge variations between all the different ales that can be brewed. Incorporate nontraditional ingredients into the mix and the possibilities are endless.

IMPERIAL PALE ALE

The pale ale style originated in the United Kingdom and the fruity, estery profile of these beers was gained, in part by the mineral-rich water found in the regions where it was brewed. American craft brewing traditions have often revolved around taking storied continental styles and amplifying the flavors and alcohol components to make for bigger, more robust beers. The following recipe celebrates this new-world tradition.

INGREDIENTS

Preboil tea

4 1/2 gallons (17 L) water

Grain bag

1 pound (455 g) 60 Lovibond Crystal malt

2 teaspoons (28 g) gypsum

Boil

8 pounds (3.6 kg) pale liquid malt extract or 6½ pounds (3 kg) dry light malt extract *(65 minutes)*

1 1/2 ounces (43 g) Centennial hops (bittering) *(60 minutes)*

1 teaspoon (5 g) Irish Moss *(20 minutes)*

1 ounce (28 g) Cascade hops (flavoring) *(10 minutes)*

1/2 ounce (15 g) Cascade hops (aroma) *(End of boil)*

In carboy

Cool water to the 5-gallon (19-L) mark

Fermentation

Yeast: Wyeast 1056 or 1272; or White Labs WLP001 or WLP051; Safale US-05

1/2 pound (225 g) light brown sugar *(Day 2)*

Dry Hop

1 ounce (28 g) Cascade hops *(Days 5–7)*

Bottling

5 ounces (140 g) priming sugar

STARTING GRAVITY: 1.069

FINAL GRAVITY: 1.014

FINAL TARGET alcohol by volume (ABV): 8.5%

PROCESS

1. Place the crushed crystal malt in the grain bag. Tie off the top and place the bag in the brewpot filled with 4½-gallons (17 L) of cool water. Add the gypsum. Heat the pot, and stir the water and grain bag every 5 minutes.

2. Just as the water reaches 170°F (77°C), pull the grain bag out of the water using a large stirring spoon. Hold the bag above the brewpot for a minute allowing most of the liquid to drain into the pot. Do not squeeze the grain bag.

3. As the water begins to boil, remove the pot from the heat. Add the pale malt extract. Stir to prevent clumping and scorching on the bottom of the pot. Return the pot to the heat.

4. Allow the wort to come up to a boil. After preboiling for 5 minutes add the Centennial bittering hops and stir. Start timing the 1-hour boil at the point that you make this hop addition.

5. 20 minutes from the end of the boil, add the Irish moss and stir for 1 minute.

6. 10 minutes before the end of the boil, add the Cascade flavoring hops and stir for 1 minute.

7. At the 60-minute mark (end of boil), add the Cascade aroma hops, stir for 1 minute, and turn off heat source. Stir the wort clockwise for 2 minutes as you build up a whirlpool effect. Stop stirring and allow the wort to sit for 10 minutes.

8. Chill the wort in a cold water bath to a temperature of 70°F–75°F (21°C–24°C).

9. Transfer the wort into fermenter; aerate for 1 minute.

10. Top up the wort to the 5-gallon (19 L) level with cold water.

11. Pitch the yeast into the carboy and aerate for another minute.

12. After fermentation takes off (1 or 2 days), add the light brown sugar to the fermenter by dissolving it in 2 cups (470 ml) of boiling water.

13. Once fermentation is over (no more bubbling in the air lock), add the Cascade hops for dry hopping.

14. In about 10 days, your beer should be ready to package.

15. Before bottling, clean and sanitize bottles and caps and create a priming solution of 1 cup (235 ml) boiling water and priming sugar. Siphon the beer into a sterilized bottling bucket, add the water-diluted priming solution, and gently stir. Bottle and cap the beer.

16. Allow the beer to bottle condition for about 2 weeks, and it should then be ready to drink.

DARK STAR LICORICE STOUT

A stout is a very dark ale that has a more assertive roasty malt character than a porter. The dark grains used in brewing this beer tend to give it a relatively bitter taste profile. Licorice root contains a natural acid called *glycyrrhizin*, which is quite sweet, even in small doses. This will act as a pleasant counterbalance to the bitterness of the dark barley.

INGREDIENTS

Preboil tea

4¹/2 gallons (17 L) water

Grain bag

9 ounces (125 g) crushed black patent malt

6 ounces (85 g) crushed roasted barley malt

2 teaspoons (10 g) gypsum

Boil

9.9 pounds (4.5 kg) dark liquid malt extract or 8 pounds (3.6 kg) of dark dry malt extract *(65 minutes)*

1 pound (455 g) light dry malt extract *(65 minutes)*

3 ounces (85 g) Fuggles hop pellets (bittering) *(60 minutes)*

1 ounce (28 g) licorice root shredded into small pieces *(20 minutes)*

1 teaspoon (5 g) Irish moss *(20 minutes)*

1/2 ounce (15 g) Willamette hop pellets *(10 minutes)*

1/2 ounce (7 g) Fuggles hop pellets (aroma) *(End of boil)*

In carboy

Cool water to the 5-gallon (19-L) mark

Fermentation

Yeast: White Labs WLP004/1084 Irish Ale Yeast; WLP001/1056 American Ale Yeast; or Safale US-05

Bottling

5 ounces (140 g) priming sugar

STARTING GRAVITY: 1.084

FINAL GRAVITY: 1.020

FINAL TARGET ABV: 8%

PROCESS

1. Fill a grain bag with the crushed black patent malt and the crushed roasted barley. Tie off the top and place the bag in your brewpot filled with 4 1/2 gallons (17 L) of cool water. Heat the pot, and stir the water and grain bag every 5 minutes.

2. Just as the water reaches 170°F (77°C), pull out the grain bag using a large stirring spoon. Hold the bag above the brewpot for a minute, allowing most of liquid to drain into the pot. Do not squeeze the grain bag.

3. As the water begins to boil, remove the pot from the heat. Add all the malt extract. Stir well to prevent clumping and scorching on the bottom of the pot. Return the pot to heat.

4. Allow the wort to come up to a boil. After preboiling for 5 minutes, add the Fuggles bittering hop pellets and stir. Start timing the 1-hour boil at the point that you make this hop addition.

5. 20 minutes before the end of the boil, add the chunks of licorice root and Irish moss. Stir for 1 minute.

6. 10 minutes before the end of the boil, add the Willamette hop pellets and stir for 1 minute.

7. At the 60-minute mark, add the Fuggles aroma hop pellets, stir for 1 minute, and turn off heat source. Stir wort clockwise for 2 minutes as you build up a whirlpool effect. Stop stirring and allow wort to sit for 10 minutes.

8. Chill the wort in a cold water bath to a temperature of 70°F–75°F (21°C–24°C).

9. Transfer the wort into carboy. Aerate for 1 minute.

10. Pitch the yeast into the fermenter and aerate for another minute. Top up the carboy to the 5-gallon (19-L) mark with cool water.

11. In about 10 days, your beer should be ready to package.

12. Before bottling, clean and sanitize bottles and caps and create a priming solution of 1 cup (235 ml) boiling water and priming sugar. Siphon the beer into a sterilized bottling bucket, add the water-diluted priming solution, and gently stir. Bottle and cap the beer.

13. Allow the beer to bottle condition for another 10 days, and it should then be ready to drink.

BLOOD ORANGE HEFEWEIZEN

INGREDIENTS

Preboil tea

4 gallons (15 L) water

Boil

6.6 pounds (3 kg) light liquid wheat
    extract (55% wheat malt and 45%
    barley malt) *(65 minutes)*

1/2 ounce (15 g) Hallertau hop pellets
    (60 minutes)

1/2 ounce (15 g) Saaz hop pellets
    (20 minutes)

4 average sized blood oranges
    (20 minutes in another pot)

1/2 ounce (15 g) Hallertau hop pellets
    (10 minutes)

In carboy

Cool water to the 5-gallon (19-L) mark

Fermentation

Yeast: Wyeast 3068 or 3638; or White
    Labs WLP300, WLP320 or WLP380
    or Fermenting Safebrew W306
    or T58

Bottling

5 ounces (140 g) priming sugar

STARING GRAVITY: 1.050

FINAL GRAVITY: 1.12

FINAL TARGET ABV: 4.8%

H efeweizen is a centuries-old German style wheat beer that has become one of the most popular styles adapted by small commercial brewers today. Because it is light, refreshing, and thirst quenching, it is traditionally drunk in the summer months, although it has become a year-round staple of many commercial and homebrewers. The grain bill (the list of grain ingredients) for hefeweizens usually calls for half barley and half wheat. Hefeweizen beers are typically lightly hopped to allow the wheat and yeast characters to shine through. It's important to use a traditional German weissbier yeast and to ferment at slightly warmer temperatures if possible. Both the yeast strain and the warmer fermentation temperature will contribute the estery, fruity character so typical of hefeweizens. This recipe will magnify the traditional fruit profile of this style with the addition of blood orange meat and peels. The pectin in the fruit will make this beer a bit more cloudy, which is fine since the style is characteristically cloudy due to the wheat.

PROCESS

1. Heat 4 gallons (15 L) of water in the brewpot. As the water begins to boil, remove it from heat. Add the light wheat malt extract. Stir to prevent clumping and scorching on the bottom of the pot. Return the pot to heat.

2. Allow the wort to come up to a boil. After pre-boiling for 5 minutes, add the first Hallertau hop pellets and stir. Start timing the 1-hour boil at the point that you make this hop addition.

3. 20 minutes before the end of the boil, add the Saaz hop pellets.

4. Peel the blood oranges and separate sections of fruit. Discard half of the peels. Cut the remainder of peel and fruit sections into small pieces. Use a grater as you only want the orange part of the rind. The white will add extreme bitterness. They should be small enough to allow easy entry into the carboy in a later step. An alternative is to use a plastic fermentation bucket that would allow easier addition of the fruit. When using a plastic fermenter with a large lid, the size of the fruit is not a concern.
The fruit may be placed in a straining bag for easy removal after fermentation. Heat fruit and peels in 1/2 gallon (2 L) of water to 160°F (71°C) and then turn off heat. Let it steep as it cools.

5. 10 minutes before the end of the boil, add the second Hallertau hop pellets and stir for 1 minute.

6. At the 60-minute mark, turn off the heat source. Stir the wort clockwise for 2 minutes as you build up a whirlpool effect. Stop stirring and allow the wort to sit for 10 minutes.

7. Chill the wort in a cold water bath to a temperature of 70°F–75°F (21°C–24°C).

8. Transfer the wort into a carboy or a plastic fermenter. Pour blood orange peels and fruit into the wort.

9. Aerate for 1 minute.

10. Pitch the yeast into the carboy and aerate for another minute. Top up the carboy to a 5-gallon (19 L) mark with cool water.

11. In about 10 days, your beer should be ready to package.

12. Before bottling, clean and sanitize bottles and caps and create a priming solution of 1 cup (235 ml) boiling water and priming sugar. Siphon the beer into a sterilized bottling bucket, add the water-diluted priming solution, and gently stir. Bottle and cap the beer.

13. Allow the beer to bottle condition for another 10 days, and it should then be ready to drink.

GINGER SAISON

INGREDIENTS

Preboil tea

4 1/2 gallons water (17 L)

1 pound (455 g) crushed Cara-Munich barley

Grain bag

2 teaspoons (10 g) gypsum

Boil

6.6 pounds (3 kg) light liquid malt extract *(65 minutes)*

1 pound (455 g) light dry malt extract *(65 minutes)*

 (or 6 pounds [2.1 kg] light dry malt extract)

1 1/2 ounces (43 g) Hallertau hop pellets
   (bittering) *(60 minutes)*

1 pound (455 g) light Belgian candi sugar *(15 minutes)*

1/2 ounce (15 g) Hallertau hop pellets (flavor) *(10 minutes)*

1 teaspoon (5 g) Irish moss *(10 minutes)*

1/2 ounce (15 g) Styrian Golding hop pellets (aroma)
   (5 minutes)

4 ounces (115 g) crystallized ginger cut into pea size
   pieces *(End of boil)*

In carboy

Cool water to 5-gallon (19-L) mark

Fermentation

Yeast: Wyeast 3724 Saison, 3725 Biere de Garde,
   3726 Farm House Ale; or White Labs WLP565
   Saison

Bottling

5 ounces (140 g) priming sugar

STARTING GRAVITY: 1.072

FINAL GRAVITY: 1.015

FINAL TARGET ABV: 7%

Saisons are traditional Belgian farmhouse-style ales that are relatively light in body and color. They are usually dry and spicy from the Belgian ale yeast, and contain a healthy dose of hops. They also tend to be a bit stronger in alcohol than the average beer. This version will get some additional fermentable sugars from the use of light Belgian candi (beet) sugar and the spiciness will be enhanced with a bit of crystallized ginger root.

PROCESS

1. Fill a grain bag with the crushed Cara-Munich barley. Tie off the top and place the bag in the brewpot filled with 4 1/2 (17 L) gallons of cool water. Add the gypsum to the water. Heat the pot, and stir the water and grain bag every 5 minutes.

2. As the water begins to reach 170°F (77°C), pull out the grain bag using a large stirring spoon. Hold the bag above the brewpot for a minute, allowing most of the liquid to drain into the pot. Do not squeeze the grain bag.

3. As the water begins to boil, remove the pot from the heat. Add all the malt extract (liquid and/or dry). Stir to prevent clumping and scorching on the bottom of the pot. Return the pot to heat.

4. Allow the wort to come up to a boil. After preboiling for 5 minutes, add the bittering Hallertau hop pellets and stir. Start timing the 1-hour boil at the point that you make this hop addition.

5. 15 minutes before the end of the boil, add the Belgian candi sugar. Stir until all of the candi sugar is dissolved into the wort.

6. 10 minutes before the end of the boil, add the flavoring Hallertau hop pellets and the Irish moss, and stir for 1 minute.

7. 5 minutes before the end of the boil, add the aroma Styrian Golding hop pellets, and stir for 1 minute.

8. At the 60-minute mark, add the cup of crystallized ginger, stir for 1 minute, and turn off heat source. Stir wort clockwise for 2 minutes as you build up a whirlpool effect. Stop stirring and allow the wort to sit for 10 minutes.

9. Chill the wort in a cold water bath to a temperature of 70°F–75°F (21°C–24°C).

10. Transfer the wort into the fermenter, aerate for 1 minute.

11. Pitch the yeast into the carboy and aerate for another minute. Top up the carboy to the 5-gallon (19-L) mark with cool water. Ferment at 68° to 80° F (20° to 27° C). The higher temperature will accentuate the characteristics of these Belgium yeasts.

12. In about 10 days, your beer should be ready to package.

13. Before bottling, clean and sanitize bottles and caps and create a priming solution of 1 cup (235 ml) boiling water and priming sugar. Siphon the beer into a sterilized bottling bucket, add the water-diluted priming solution, and gently stir. Bottle and cap the beer.

14. Allow the beer to bottle condition for another 10 days, and it should then be ready to drink.

TRIPEL 'ROUND THE WORLD

Tripel Round can best be described as a traditional strong, pale, Belgian–style ale on an exotic road trip. In most instances, the malt sugars in Belgian tripel ales are augmented with white, brown, or candi sugar. For this version, you will venture to the Far East (or at least an Asian grocery store) for Chinese rock sugar. Usually used to braise meats, this sugar is a mixture of refined sugar, brown sugar, and honey that has a subtle pleasant spiciness. For a finishing touch, add a bit of dried chamomile to give a fruity finish that will complement the estery profile of the Belgian yeast. A vigorous yeast strain will be needed to ferment this strong brew.

INGREDIENTS

Preboil tea

4 1/2 gallons (17 L) cool water

1 pound (455 g) crushed Cara-pils barley

Grain bag

2 teaspoons (10 g) gypsum

Boil

9.9 pounds (4.5 kg) light liquid malt extract plus 1 pound (455 g) light dry malt extract; or 8 pounds (3.6 kg) light dry malt extract *(65 minutes)*

1 ounce (28 g) Saaz hop pellets (bittering) *(60 minutes)*

1 pound (455 g) Chinese rock sugar *(30 minutes)*

1 teaspoon (5 g) Irish moss *(20 minutes)*

1 ounce (28 g) East Kent Golding hop pellets (flavor) *(20 minutes)*

1/2 ounce (15 g) Saaz hop pellets (aroma) *(10 minutes)*

1 pound (455 g) Chinese rock sugar *(5 minutes)*

1 1/2 ounces (43 g) dried chamomile *(End of boil)*

In carboy

Cool water to the 5 gallon (19-L) mark

Fermentation

Yeast: Wyeast 1762 Belgian Abbey Yeast or 3787 Trappist High Gravity; or White Labs WLP530 or WLP575

1 pound (455) light brown sugar *(Day 2)*

Bottling

5 ounces (140 g) priming sugar

STARTING GRAVITY: 1.090

FINAL GRAVITY: 1.018

FINAL TARGET ABV: 9%

PROCESS

1. Fill a grain bag with the crushed Cara-pils malt. Tie off the top and place the bag in the brewpot filled with 4^1/$_2$ gallons (17 L) of cool water. Add the gypsum. Heat the pot, and stir the water and grain bag every 5 minutes.

2. When the water reaches 170°F (77°C), pull out the grain bag using a large stirring spoon. Hold the bag above the brewpot for a minute, allowing most of the liquid to drain into the pot. Do not squeeze the grain bag.

3. As the water begins to boil, remove the pot from the heat. Add all the malt extract. Stir to prevent clumping and scorching on the bottom of the pot. Return the brewpot to the heat.

4. Allow the wort to come to a boil. After preboiling for 5 minutes, add the Saaz hop pellets for bittering and stir. Start timing the 1-hour boil at the point that you make this hop addition.

5. 30 minutes before the end of the boil, add 1 of the 2 pounds (455 g) of Chinese rock sugar, and stir for a minute.

6. 20 minutes before the end of the boil, add the East Kent Golding hop pellets and the Irish moss, and stir for 1 minute.

7. 10 before the end of the boil, add the aroma Saaz hop pellets, and stir for 1 minute.

8. Five minutes before the end of the boil, add the last pound (455 g) of Chinese rock sugar, and stir for 1 minute.

9. At the 60-minute mark, add the dried chamomile. Stir for 1 minute, and turn off the heat source. Stir the wort clockwise for 2 minutes as you build up a whirlpool effect. Stop stirring and allow the wort to sit for 10 minutes.

10. Chill the wort in a cold-water bath to a temperature of 70°F–75°F (21°C–24°C).

11. Transfer the wort with the chamomile into the carboy. Aerate for 1 minute.

12. Top up the carboy with cool water to the 5-gallon (19-L) mark and aerate for another minute.

13. Pitch the yeast into the carboy. (See yeast starter directions on page 65.)

14. After fermentation takes off (1 or 2 days), bring 2 cups (470 ml) of water to a boil, and add the brown sugar. When dissolved, add this to the fermenting beer in the carboy.

15. In about 10 days, your beer should be ready to package.

16. Before bottling, clean and sanitize bottles and caps and create a priming solution of 1 cup (235 ml) boiling water and priming sugar. Siphon the beer into a sterilized bottling bucket, add the water-diluted priming solution, and gently stir. Bottle and cap the beer.

17. Allow the beer to bottle condition for another 2 weeks, and it should then be ready to drink.

KIWIT

INGREDIENTS

Preboil tea

4¹/2 gallons (17 L) cool watr

¹/2 pound (225 g) Torrified wheat grain

¹/2 pound (225 g) 6 row pale malt

Grain bag

2 teaspoons (10 g) gypsum

Boil

6.6 pounds (3 kg) wheat-barley liquid malt extract *(65 minutes)*

(or 5 pounds [2.3 kg] dry wheat malt extract)

1 ounce (28 g) Tettnanger hop pellets *(60 minutes)*

¹/2 ounce (15 g) Willamette hop pellets *(10 minutes)*

¹/2 ounce (15 g) crushed coriander *(10 minutes)*

1 teaspoon (5 g) Irish moss *(10 minutes)*

4 pounds (1.8 kg) fresh kiwi fruit peeled and cubed (¹/2 inch [1.27 cm] cubes) *(End of boil)*

In carboy

Cool water to 5-gallon (19-L) mark

Fermentation

Yeast: White Labs WLP400 Belgian Wit Ale or WLP410 Belgian Wit II; or Wyeast 3944 Belgian Wit or 3463 Forbidden Fruit or Safale S-33

Bottling

5 ounces (140 g) priming sugar

STARTING GRAVITY: 1.052

FINAL GRAVITY: 1.014

FINAL TARGET ABV: 5%

Wit, or white, beers are traditional Belgian beers made with wheat and a variety of spices. They are relatively light in body and alcohol, and are very refreshing. The style dates back to before hops were domestically grown, and brewers were forced to spice or bitter their beer with whatever ingredients were handy. Modern wit beers are usually spiced with Curaçao orange peel and crushed coriander. Since Kiwi is such a refreshing tropical fruit, it works well with a wit style beer; in this recipe, the coriander will remain but Kiwi will replace the orange peel. Make sure the fresh kiwis you find for this beer are nice and firm and not mushy and browning. Soak them in hot water for a few minutes and it should be easier to peel the skin off of them.

PROCESS

1. Mix the grains together before filling a grain bag with the crushed 6 row pale malt and the crushed Torrified wheat. Torrified grains are heated to make the grain pop similar to puffed rice or wheat to explode the cell walls. It makes the interior of the grain more usable for the brewing process. Tie off the top and place the bag in the brewpot filled with 4¹/2 gallons (17 L) of cool water. Add the gypsum to the water. Heat the pot and stir the water and grain bag every few minutes.

2. When the water reaches 170°F (77°C), pull out the grain bag using a large stirring spoon. Hold the bag above the brewpot for a minute, allowing most of the liquid to drain into the pot. Do not squeeze the grain bag.

3. As the water begins to boil, remove the pot from the heat. Add the wheat-barley malt extract. Stir to prevent clumping and scorching on the bottom of the pot. Return the pot to the heat.

4. Allow the wort to come up to a boil. After preboiling for 5 minutes, add the Tettnanger bittering hop pellets and stir. Start timing the 1-hour boil at the point that you make this hop addition.

5. 10 minutes before the end of the boil, add the Willamette hop pellets, coriander and Irish moss, and stir for 1 minute.

6. At the 60-minute mark in the boil, add the cubed kiwi fruit, and shut off the heat source. Stir the wort clockwise for 2 minutes as you build up a whirlpool effect. Stop stirring and allow the wort to sit for 20 minutes.

7. Chill the wort in a cold water bath to a temperature of 70°F–75°F (21°C–24°C). Transfer the wort and fruit into the carboy, and aerate for 1 minute.

8. Pitch the yeast into the carboy or bucket and aerate for another minute. Top up the fermenter with cool water to the 5-gallon (19-L) mark.

9. Primary fermentation will take a little longer than usual (this beer should be done fermenting in 15 to 20 days). When the kiwis rise to the top of the carboy and are almost white in color, this will signify that they have been successfully stripped of their flavors and sugars.

10. Before bottling, clean and sanitize bottles and caps and create a priming solution of 1 cup (235 ml) boiling water and priming sugar. Siphon the beer into a sterilized bottling bucket, add the water-diluted priming solution, and gently stir. Bottle and cap the beer.

11. After bottling, allow the beer to bottle condition for another 10 days; it should then be ready to drink.

CHAPTER 7

Extreme Lagers

WHEN IT COMES TO brewing lagers, there has been significantly less experimentation in the commercial and homebrewing worlds than there has been with ales. Part of the reason for this is that it's more difficult to achieve ideal fermenting temperatures with lagers than it is with ales. But I think the history of lager brewing plays a role in this reality as well. The German Purity Act mandates that beer can be made with ONLY yeast, hops, barley, wheat, and water. This militant position has affected the lager culture in a way that stifled creative brewing with non-traditional ingredients. As homebrewers and commercial brewers outside of Germany are not obligated to obey the Purity Act, experimentation with lager brewing is on the rise. Extreme lagers are as easy and as much fun to brew as extreme ales. However, as lagers ferment from the bottom up at cooler temperatures, you'll need a bit more patience and access to a cooler area in order to ferment them. The extreme lager recipes in this chapter acknowledge the genesis of the styles, but incorporate extreme ingredients and techniques.

Lager Temperatures

Ale yeasts ferment from the top down in ideal temperatures of around 70°F (21°C), and lager yeasts ferment from the bottom up in ideal temperatures of around 50°F (10°C). Because commercial breweries use brewing tanks that have cooling coils or jackets to regulate temperature, there is less challenge with maintaining proper lager temperatures. Your homebrewing carboy does not have a temperature-control system. For this reason, many homebrewers tend to brew lagers in the cooler months when cellar or garage temperatures are between 40°F and 50°F (4°C–10°C). The easiest way to ferment lagers at the proper temperature, without having to wait around for

Refrigerator Conversion

Doug Griffith, XtremeBrewing.com

I HAVE FOUND THAT a consistent fermentation temperature of about 68°F (20°C) makes ales taste better. I prefer the lower end of the recommended fermenting temperatures, as I've found that those temperatures work well with most ale yeasts for beers of normal gravity. To me, it is one of the main variables in brewing that most helps consistency. A few years ago, I was only making ales and in order to maintain a consistently cool temperature during

the warmer months, I acquired an old refrigerator. I thought that I would be able to plug it in, adjust the thermostat for a temperature about 68°F (20°C) and be ready to ferment. Well, it wasn't quite that easy. I found that the thermostats in most refrigerators are not designed to be set for anything above 40°F (4°C); they're designed to keep food cold, not cool. After moving the heavy unit, I was determined to make it work. I discovered that an external temperature controller, available at most homebrew stores, would do exactly what I needed.

The temperature controller is a device that sits or hangs on the outside of the refrigerator. The refrigerator power cord usually plugs into the backside of the temperature controller power cord. The controller has an attached temperature sensor tube that's about 3 feet (90 cm) long and gets placed inside the refrigerator. Most of the sensor tubing is about 1/8 inch (3 mm) in diameter and easily runs under the door seal to the interior of the refrigerator. Some controllers have sensors designed to be inserted into your brew in the fermenter for

Mother Nature, is to convert an old refrigerator into a fermenting place. This will take some space and money but is quite effective. Look in the classified ads for a cheap but functioning used refrigerator. Once you have a suitable unit, remove the top shelves. This will create space to store your carboy comfortably and safely in the bottom of the refrigerator. Plug in the refrigerator, set the thermostat for 48°F (9°C) and wait a few hours to see if the temperature in the refrigerator will stabilize there. Most refrigerators will not control the temperature above 40°F (4°C). If this is the case with your refrigerator, an external temperature controller will be required. These are available from most homebrew stores.

optimal accuracy. Two types of controllers are available: digital display and dial. Both are sufficiently accurate. The digital display units usually have some additional features (direct-read temperature on the display and adjustable high and low temperature differential), but either will work well. When using a dial type, a thermometer inside the refrigerator helps to confirm the correct temperature setting. I set the temperature to the desired setting and put my wort inside to ferment. Now that I had a space where I could control my temperature between about 34°F (1°C) (the coldest the refrigerator fermentation space will get) and 80°F (27°C) (the warmest the temperature controller will control), I have been doing two or three lagers a year. I still like the shorter turnaround time of the ales, but many of my friends enjoy the crisp, clean taste of a lager occasionally. I make my lagers during the winter using the refrigerator and temperature controller and, at the same time, I can ferment my ales in a cool area in my house. When it starts getting warm, I usually go back to using the refrigerator for my ales. Originally, I thought that I would be able to use my newly acquired refrigerator for storing and dispensing my finished brews, because I now put most of my beers in corny kegs to force-carbonate and dispense. But I found that it was difficult to juggle between finished product and fermenting. I now have a second refrigerator for dispensing, but that is another story. I am extremely pleased with my fermenting refrigerator setup, the consistency it provides, and the fact that I can now do lagers.

IMPERIAL PILSNER

A good pilsner is quite pale in color, with a pronounced malt character. Its hop profile, however, is further forward than the malt in both taste and aroma. This recipe will be a true all-barley version of the style. In order to bring this rendition into the realm of the extreme, significantly more barley and hops than the average pilsner calls for will be used. Since lager beers require more aging time than ales, you will need to transfer this beer to the sterilized bottling bucket, clean and sanitize the carboy, then transfer it back into the carboy on more hops for aging. By adding the hops after fermentation is complete, the beer will maintain more of the wonderful hop aromas that would have dissipated with the CO_2 gas had the hops been added during the height of primary fermentation. You may even want to goose this pilsner with more hop complexity by preparing the bottle-conditioning priming sugar as a hop tea.

INGREDIENTS

Preboil tea

4 gallons (15 L) cool water

1/2 pound (225 g) Cara-pils crushed malt

2 teaspoons (10 g) gypsum

Boil

8 pounds (3.6 kg) Pilsner or light liquid malt extract *(65 minutes)*

3 pounds (1.4 kg) extra light dry malt extract *(65 minutes)*

 (or 9.5 pounds [4.3 kg] Pilsner extra light dry malt extract)

1 ounce (28 g) Saaz hop pellets (Bittering) *(60 minutes)*

1/2 ounce (15 g) Saaz hop pellets (Flavor) *(20 minutes)*

1/2 ounce (7 g) Saaz hop pellet (aroma) *(10 minutes)*

 1 teaspoon (5 g) Irish moss *(10 minutes)*

1/2 ounce (7 g) Saaz hop pellets (aroma) *(End of boil)*

Dry hopping

1 ounce (28 g) whole-leaf Hallertau hops *(2 to 3 weeks)*

In carboy

Cold water to 5-gallon (19-L) mark

Fermentation

Yeast: Wyeast 2035 American Lager or 2124 Bohemian Lager; White Labs WLP840 or WLP830 or Saflager S-23 or S-34/70

Bottling

1 ounce (28 g) whole-leaf Hallertau hops (final hop tea)

5 ounces (140 g) priming sugar

STARTING GRAVITY: 1.089

FINAL GRAVITY: 1.016

FINAL TARGET ABV: 9%

PROCESS

1. Fill a single grain bag with the crushed Cara-pils malt. Tie off the top and place the bag in the brewpot filled with 4 gallons (15 L) of cool water. Add the gypsum. Heat the pot, and stir the water and grain bag every 5 minutes.

2. As the water reaches 170°F (77°C), pull out the grain bag using a large stirring spoon. Hold the bag above the brewpot for a minute, allowing most of the liquid to drain into the pot. Do not squeeze the grain bag.

3. As the water begins to boil, remove the pot from the heat. Add the lager malt extract syrup and dry malt extract. Stir to prevent clumping and scorching on the bottom of the pot. Return the pot to the heat.

4. Allow the wort to come up to a boil. After preboiling for 5 minutes, add the bittering Saaz hop pellets and stir. Start timing the 1-hour boil at the point that you make this hop addition.

5. 20 minutes before the end of the boil, add the flavoring Saaz hop pellets.

6. 10 minutes before the end of the 1-hour boil, put in the third Saaz hop pellets addition and the Irish moss, and stir for 1 minute.

7. At the 60-minute mark of the boil, add the last of the Saaz hops and remove the pot from the heat source. Stir the wort clockwise for 2 minutes as you build up a whirlpool effect. Stop stirring and allow the wort to sit for 10 minutes.

8. Chill the wort in a cold water bath to just below 55°F (13°C). Use some ice in the water bath to help cool the wort to the lager fermentation temperature.

9. Transfer the wort into the carboy. Aerate for 1 minute.

10. Pitch the yeast into the carboy and aerate for another minute. Top up with water to 5 gallons (19 L).

11. Store the carboy in a cool place (at or under 50°F [10°C]) for the duration of fermentation.

12. After primary fermentation is complete (about 2 to 3 weeks), transfer the wort into a sanitized bottling bucket and then sanitize your now-empty carboy. A hydrometer gravity of around 1.015 will indicate that primary fermentation is complete. Place 1 ounce (28 g) of whole-leaf Hallertau hops in a grain bag, and make sure it's well sealed. Push the grain bag through the neck of the empty carboy before transferring your beer back into it. If possible, reduce the temperature to around 40°F (4°C) for the extended lagering (storage).

13. In about 2 or 3 weeks, your beer should be ready to package.

14. On bottling day, boil 6 ounces (175 ml) of water and add the sugar and the final Hallertau hops. Let it steep for a good 20 minutes before straining it through a cheesecloth-lined colander (to catch the hop leafs and solids) on its way into your bottling bucket.

15. Before bottling, clean and sanitize bottles and caps and create a priming solution of 1 cup (235 ml) boiling water and priming sugar. Siphon the beer into a sterilized bottling bucket, add the water-diluted priming solution, and gently stir.

16. Allow the beer to bottle condition for about 2 weeks, and it should then be ready to drink

PEPPERCORN RYE-BOCK

INGREDIENTS

Preboil tea

4¹/₂ gallons (17 L) cool water

1 pound (455 g) flaked rye

¹/₂ pound (225 g) crushed Munich malt

Grain bag

Boil

6.6 pounds (3 kg) pilsner or light liquid malt extract *(65 minutes)*

1 pound (455 g) light dry malt extract *(65 minutes)*

  (or 6 pounds [2.7 kg] extra light dry malt extract)

1 ounce (28 g) cluster hop pellets *(60 minutes)*

1 ounce (28 g) Hallertau hop pellets *(10 minutes)*

1 teaspoon (5 g) Irish moss *(10 minutes)*

1 teaspoon (2 g) milled black peppercorns *(End of boil)*

1 teaspoon (2 g) milled green peppercorns *(End of boil)*

In carboy

Cold water to the 5-gallon (19-L) mark

Fermentation

Yeast: Wyeast 2308 Munich or 2206 Bavarian Lager; or White Labs WLP838 Southern German Lager yeast

Saflager S-23 or S-34/70

Bottling

5 ounces (140 g) priming sugar

STARTING GRAVITY: 1.063

FINAL GRAVITY: 1.014

FINAL TARGET ABV: 5.5%

The bock beer style has been made in Northern Germany and Austria for centuries. The Dutch version of a bock beer is usually a bit darker in color than those from other countries, and there is evidence that the Dutch used rye in making some versions of their bock beers. Bock beers tend to lean more on the barley than the hops for their signature character. The rye that will be used in this recipe will give the beer a nice, spicy, woody edge to cut the sweetness of the barley. Black and green peppercorns will be added to further accentuate the spicy notes in this beer.

PROCESS

1. Fill a single grain bag with the flaked rye and Munich malt. Tie off the top and place the bag in your brewpot filled with 4¹/₂ (17 L) gallons of cool water. Heat the pot, and stir the water and grain bag every 5 minutes.

2. As the water reaches 170°F (77°C), pull out the grain bag using a large stirring spoon. Hold the bag above the brewpot for a minute, allowing most of the liquid to drain into the pot. Do not squeeze the grain bag.

3. As the water begins to boil, remove the pot from the heat. Add all the malt extract. Stir to prevent clumping and scorching on the bottom of the pot. Return the pot to the heat.

4. Allow the wort to come up to a boil. After preboiling for 5 minutes, add the cluster hop pellets and stir. Start timing the 1-hour boil at the point that you make this hop addition.

6. 10 minutes before the end of the 1-hour boil, add the Hallertau hop pellets and the Irish moss, and stir for 1 minute.

7. At the 60-minute mark, add the black and green peppercorns, and turn off the heat source. Stir the wort clockwise for 2 minutes as you build up a whirl-pool effect. Stop stirring and allow the wort to sit for 10 minutes.

8. Chill the wort in a cold water bath to a temperature of under 55°F (13°C).

9. Transfer the wort into the carboy, and aerate for 1 minute.

10. Pitch the yeast into the carboy, and aerate for another minute. Top up with water to 5 gallons (19 L).

11. Store in a cool place (at or under 50°F [10°C]) for the duration of fermentation.

12. After primary fermentation is complete (about 2 to 3 weeks), trans-fer the wort into a sanitized bottling bucket, and then sanitize your now-empty carboy. Variation: Place 1 oz (28 g) whole-leaf Hallertau hops in a grain bag and make sure it is well sealed. Push grain bag through the neck of the sanitized carboy.

13. In about 2 more weeks, your beer should be ready to package.

14. Before bottling, clean and sanitize bottles and caps, and create a priming solution of 1 cup (235 ml) boiling water and priming sugar. Siphon the beer into a sterilized bottling bucket, add the priming sugar solution, and gently stir. Fill bottles 1" to 1½" (2.5 to 3.8 cm) from the top and cap.

15. Allow the beer to bottle condition for another 2 weeks, and it should then be ready to drink.

Variation for priming sugar: On bottling day, boil 12 oz (355 ml) water and 5 oz (140 g) priming sugar. Let the temperature of the priming sugar solution drop to about 160°F (71°C) then place 1 oz (28 g) Hallertau leaf hops in a hop bag and put in the pot and cover. Let it steep for 20 minutes before removing the bagged hops. Add to bottling bucket and stir gently.

MOLASSES MARZEN

Marzen beers are German in heritage, have a relatively sweet malt character, and tend to have a reddish hue. Traditionally, Marzen beers were brewed in the spring to lager through the warm summer months. This method was the result of brewing these beers in the days before modern refrigeration. After fermentation, the beers were transferred into barrels and rolled deep into caves and cellars where they were packed with ice to age over the summer. The extended lagering time gives Marzen their smooth but crisp malt character. This Marzen will be a bit stronger than the standard 5 to 6 percent ABV continental version. To bump up the ABV to 8.5 percent, this recipe will use molasses. Brewing with molasses is a tradition that is actually more prevalent in Britain than in Germany, but allowing the worlds to collide can be a fun way to make an ordinary beer a bit more extreme. Be sure to use high-

grade, light molasses, which is about 90 percent fermentable. In addition to sugars, molasses contains aromatics that will contribute to the flavor and complexity of this beer.

INGREDIENTS

Preboil tea

4¹/₂ gallons (17 L) cool water

1 pound (455 g) 60 Lovibond Crystal malt

Grain bag

2 teaspoons (10 g) gypsum

Boil

6.6 pounds (3 kg) pilsner or light liquid malt extract *(65 minutes)*

2 pounds (900 g) light brown sugar *(65 minutes)*

1¹/₂ ounces (43 g) Chinook hop pellets *(60 minutes)*

1 teaspoon (5 g) Irish moss *(20 minutes)*

1 pound (680 g) light molasses *(20 minutes)*

1 ounce (28 g) Saaz hop pellets *(10 minutes)*

1 teaspoon (5 g) Irish moss *(10 minutes)*

In carboy

Cold water to the 5-gallon (19L) mark

Fermentation

Yeast: Wyeast 2042 Danish Lager yeast or White Labs WLP830; or Saflager S-23

Bottling

8 ounces (340 g) molasses for priming

STARTING GRAVITY: 1.080

FINAL GRAVITY: 1.016

FINAL TARGET ABV: 8%

PROCESS

1. Fill a grain bag with the crushed 60 Lovibond crystal malt. Tie off the top and place the bag in your brewpot filled with 4 1/2 (17 L) gallons of cool water. Heat the pot and stir the water and grain bag every 5 minutes.

2. As the water reaches 170°F (77°C), pull out the grain bag using a large stirring spoon. Hold the bag above the brewpot for a minute, allowing the last of liquids to drain into the pot. Do not squeeze the grain bag.

3. As the water begins to boil, remove the pot from the heat. Add the light liquid malt extract and brown sugar. Stir to prevent clumping and scorching on the bottom of the pot. Return the pot to the heat.

4. Allow the wort to come up to a boil. After preboiling for 5 minutes, add the Chinook hop pellets and stir. Start timing the 1-hour boil at the point that you make this hop addition.

5. 20 minutes before the end of your boil, add the light molasses; stir to prevent clumping.

6. 10 minutes before the end of your 1-hour boil, add the Saaz hop pellets and the Irish moss, and stir for 1 minute.

7. At the 60-minute mark, turn off your heat source. Stir the wort clockwise for 2 minutes as you build up a whirlpool effect. Stop stirring and allow the wort to sit for 10 minutes.

8. Chill the wort in a cold water bath to just below 55°F (13°C).

9. Transfer the wort into the carboy, and aerate for 1 minute.

10. Pitch the yeast into the carboy, and aerate for another minute. Top up with water to 5 gallons (19 L).

11. Store in a cool place (at or under 50°F [10°C]) for the duration of fermentation. In about 4 weeks, your beer should be ready to package.

12. On bottling day, boil 6 ounces (175 ml) of water and 1 cup (235 ml) of light molasses. Stir until the molasses is completely mixed into the solution. Pour it into bottling bucket and transferring the beer into it. Stir to mix well. The beer is now ready to bottle.

13. Allow the beer to bottle condition for another 2 weeks, and it should then be ready to drink.

CHAPTER 8

Extremely Unique Beers

THE RECIPES IN THIS chapter are similar to those in chapters six and seven in that they incorporate specialty grains and the occasional, nontraditional ingredient; however, they include an additional step or two to make. If you are a novice homebrewer, it's advisable to cut your teeth on some of the earlier recipes before attempting one of these. They aren't necessarily much more difficult to brew than the preceding recipes, but they usually require additional time, and potentially additional equipment. If a recipe in this chapter calls for equipment above and beyond what was recommended in an earlier chapter, the items are listed after the ingredients.

PUNKIN' PORTER

Porters have been brewed in Britain and Ireland for centuries. The style is similar to a stout in color but is usually a bit lighter in alcohol content and body. Porters are also usually a bit sweeter and less roasty than a stout. This porter also has a bit more alcohol (why not?) than the garden-variety porter and will be made with both pumpkin meat and pumpkin pie spices. As with any homebrew recipe, it's always better to use natural, raw ingredients than artificial flavors. Obviously, this is a great beer to share with family and friends during the holiday season.

INGREDIENTS

Cook

1 to 2 gallons (4 to 8 L) water to cover pumpkin

2 pounds (0.9 kg) fresh pumpkin, peeled and cut into 1-inch (2.5 cm) cubes

Mash

2 teaspoons (10 g) gypsum

1/2 gallon (2 L) water

1 pound (455 g) crushed black patent malt

1 1/2 pound (680 g) crushed pale 6-row malt

Preboil tea

Water to the 4 1/2-gallon (17 L) mark

Boil

3.3 pounds (1.5 kg) light liquid malt extract *(65 minutes)*

3 pounds (1.4 kg) amber dry malt extract *(65 minutes)*

1 pound (455 g) dark dry malt extract *(65 minutes)*

1 ounce (28 g) Hallertau hop pellets (bittering) *(60 minutes)*

2 teaspoons (10 g) Irish moss *(20 minutes)*

1 ounce (28 g) Cascade hop pellets *(20 minutes)*

1/2 ounce (15 g) Hallertau hop pellets *(10 minutes)*

1 teaspoon (5 g) allspice *(5 minutes)*

1 teaspoon (5 g) cinnamon *(5 minutes)*

1 teaspoon (5 g) nutmeg *(5 minutes)*

In carboy

Water to the 5-gallon (19-L) mark

Fermentation

Yeast: White Labs WLP001 or Wyeast 1056 American Ale Yeast or Safale US-05

Bottling

5 ounces (140 g) priming sugar

Extra equipment: potato masher, food processor or blender, and a large cheesecloth-lined colander or strainer

STARTING GRAVITY: 1.078

FINAL GRAVITY: 1.014

FINAL TARGET ABV: 8%

PROCESS

1. Wash the pumpkin and cut it in half. Remove the seeds and stringy innards. Peel the outer skin and cut it into roughly 1-inch (2.5 cm) cubes. Place the cubes in the brewpot, cover them with water, and bring the pot to a low boil for 20 minutes. Mash or run the pumpkin meat through a food processor or blender. Do not discard the boiled water. Return the pumpkin to the brewpot. Note: A 30-ounce (850 g) can of plain pumpkin and 1/2 gallon (2 L) water can be substituted if a pumpkin is not available or not in season.

2. Add 1/2 gallon (2 L) cool water, the crushed black patent, and the crushed six-row malt to the brewpot mixture. The six-row malt has enzymes that are not in the crystal malts and will help convert most of the starches in the pumpkin into sugars. Heat the water to 155°F (68°C) and hold at that temperature for about 45 minutes. This process is called mashing, and on a large scale, it's how all the barley sugars are extracted from the grains for brewing beers at our brewery. Stir occasionally. After the 45-minute mash, pour the grain, pumpkin, and water mixture through the cheesecloth-lined colander or strainer into another pot, or temporarily into your fermenter. Sometimes, a strainer works well and other times the pumpkin tends to clog the strainer. You are trying to remove as much of the grain as possible. Return everything that went through the strainer to the brewpot. Top up the brewpot with more water to about 4 1/2 (17 L) gallons. Return the pot to the heat.

3. As the water begins to boil, remove the pot from the heat. Add the malt extracts (liquid and dry). Stir to prevent clumping and scorching on the bottom of the pot. Return the pot to the heat.

4. Allow the wort to come up to a boil. After preboiling for 5 minutes, add the Hallertau hop pellets and stir. Start timing the 1-hour boil at the point that you make this hop addition.

5. 20 minutes before the end of the boil, add the Cascade hops, and the Irish moss, and stir for 1 minute.

6. 10 minutes before the end of the boil, add the last of Hallertau aroma hop pellets, and stir for 1 minute. 5 minutes before the end of your boil, add the spices (allspice, cinnamon, and nutmeg), and stir for 1 minute.

7. At the 60-minute mark of the boil, turn off the heat source. Stir the wort clockwise for 2 minutes as you build up a whirlpool effect. Stop stirring and allow the wort to sit for 10 minutes.

8. Chill the wort in a cold water bath to a temperature of 70°F–75°F (21°C–24°C).

9. Transfer the wort into the carboy. Aerate for 1 minute.

10. Pitch the yeast into the carboy, and aerate for another minute. Top up with water to the 5-gallon (19-L) mark.

11. After primary fermentation is complete (about 7 days), transfer the beer into a sanitized bottling bucket and then sanitize your now-empty carboy before transferring the beer back into it. This will remove much of the sediment from the pumpkin.

12. In about 2 weeks, your beer should be ready to package.

13. Before bottling, clean and sanitize bottles and caps, and create a priming solution of 1 cup (235 ml) boiling water and priming sugar. Siphon beer into a sterilized bottling bucket, add the water-diluted priming solution, and gently stir. Bottle and cap the beer.

14. Allow the beer to bottle condition for another 10 days, and it should then be ready to drink.

SOUR CHERRY ALE

Belgian Cherry beers are called Kriek, and they are usually brewed with wild yeast and specific bacteria strains. Later recipes in this chapter will incorporate this lambic fermentation process, but this is a more straight-forward fruit beer. Because this beer is fermented with the cherry meat and pits in the fermenter, there will be some beer loss as the fruit solids absorb some of the beer. The pits will add a subtle woody character to the beer. It would be nice to have two carboys for this beer, but it is not necessary if you use your bottling bucket to transfer the beer out of the carboy (so it can be cleaned) between primary fermentation and conditioning. With its subtle red hue and excellent pairing with dark chocolate, this is a great beer for romantic occasions.

INGREDIENTS

Preboil tea

4¹/₂ gallons (17 L) cool water

8 ounces (100 g) crushed wheat malt

8 ounces (100 g) crushed Munich malt

Grain bag

2 teaspoons (10 g) gypsum

Boil

6.6 pounds (3 kg) light malt extract
(65 minutes)

1 ounce (28 g) Northern Brewer hop pellets *(60 minutes)*

¹/₂ ounce (15 g) Fuggles hop pellets
(20 minutes)

¹/₂ ounce (15 g) Tettnanger hop pellets
(10 minutes)

1 teaspoon (5 g) Irish moss *(10 minutes)*

10 pounds (4.5 kg) crushed sour red cherries, 7 (3.2 kg) pounds of cherries if using frozen or 2 pounds (900 g) dried cherries *(End of boil)*

4 teaspoons (20 g) pectic enzyme
(End of boil)

Fermentation

Yeast: Wyeast 1968 ESB or 1388 Belgian Strong Ale; or White Labs WLP002 English ale/ESB or Safale S-04

Bottling

5 ounces (140 g) priming sugar

STARTING GRAVITY: 1.066

FINAL GRAVITY: 1.016

FINAL TARGET ABV: 6.5%

PROCESS

1. Fill a grain bag with the crushed grains (Munich and wheat). Tie off the top and place the bag in the brewpot filled with 4$\frac{1}{2}$ (17 L) gallons of cool water. Add the gypsum to the water. Heat the pot, and stir the water and grain bag every 5 minutes.

2. As the water reaches 170°F (77°C), pull out the specialty grain bag using a large stirring spoon. Hold the bag above the brewpot for a minute, allowing most of the liquid to drain into the pot. Do not squeeze the grain bag.

3. As the water begins to boil, remove the pot from the heat. Add the light malt extract syrup. Stir to prevent clumping and scorching on the bottom of the pot. Return the pot to the heat.

4. Allow the wort to come up to a boil. After pre-boiling for 5 minutes, add the Northern Brewer hop pellets and stir. Start timing the 1-hour boil at the point that you make this hop addition.

5. Add the Fuggles hops 20 minutes before the end of your boil and stir for 1 minute.

6. Add the Tettnanger hop pellets and the Irish moss 10 minutes before the end of the boil, and stir for 1 minute.

7. At the 60-minute mark of the boil, turn off the heat source. Let the beer come down below 170°F (77°C). Placing the brewpot in the water bath will speed up the cooling time. Add your cherries of choice or availability. You don't want to add the fruit to boiling beer, as the high temperature will set the natural fruit pectin, which may adversely affect the taste and clarity of your beer. Stir the wort clockwise for 2 minutes as you build up a whirlpool effect. Stop stirring and allow the wort to sit for 10 minutes.

8. Chill the wort in a cold water bath until it is below 75°F (24°C).

9. For the primary fermentation, a plastic bucket fermenter would be easier to use for this brew, as it will be difficult to get the cherries in and out of the glass carboy. To aerate, pour the wort back and forth between the plastic fermenter and your sanitized bottling bucket 4 or 5 times. Add the pectic enzyme.

10. Pitch the yeast into the fermenter, and aerate for another minute. Top up to the 5-gallon (19 L) mark.

11. After primary fermentation is over (your airlock has stopped bubbling), if using the plastic fermenter, transfer your beer into the sanitized carboy, leaving behind all of the fruit, pits, and yeast solids that have settled to the bottom; if using a carboy, transfer your beer to the sanitized bottling bucket, clean the carboy and move the beer back to the carboy.

12. In about two weeks your beer should be ready to package. Rack your beer to another container to leave all sediment behind. Boil priming sugar in a cup (235 ml) of water. Add to racked beer. Stir to disperse sugar. Sanitize bottles and caps. Fill bottles 1" to 1½" (2.5 to 3.8 cm) from top and cap.

13. Allow the beer to bottle-condition for another two weeks and it should be fully carbonated.

CRANDADDY BRAGGOT

A braggot is a mixed-alcohol beverage of beer and mead. Traditional meads consist of nothing but fermented honey and water. Meads fermented with fruits or spices are called melomels. This braggot will be subtly spicy and have a pleasant fruitiness in both aroma and taste. To achieve this profile, orange blossom honey will be used for the desired citrus note. Additional fruit flavors will also be gained by adding hydrated, dried cranberries at the end of the boil. The honey won't be boiled as long as the barley extract syrup, as the boiling action drives off so many of the volatiles that give good meads their nice perfumey nose. But the honey does need to be heated for a while to gain sterility and drop out proteins that would contribute to a haze in the final braggot. Honey beers sometimes need a little prodding to complete a healthy fermentation because fewer of the yeast nutrients in barley are naturally present. For that reason, you will be adding some yeast nutrients (available from any good homebrew supply store) at the time that you pitch the yeast in the carboy. While the braggot will ferment at ale temperatures, the duration of the fermentation will probably be a bit longer than that of traditional beers. Allow a month or so before bottling.

Honeymoons?

Mead is a honey-based, fermented drink that has been enjoyed since the dark ages. In eighteenth-century England, mead was the drink of choice at weddings as it was believed to have great fertility properties. The term "honeymoon" was born from this tradition.

INGREDIENTS

Preboil

3 gallons (11 L) water

Boil

6.6 pounds (3 kg) light malt extract syrup
   (65 minutes)

1 ounce (28 g) Hallertau hop pellets
   (60 minutes)

2 pounds (900 g) dried cranberries
   (60 minutes in a separate pot)

32 ounces (950 ml) water (60 minutes in a
   separate pot)

Grain bag

1 teaspoon (5 g) Irish moss (10 minutes)

6 pounds (2.7 kg) unfiltered orange
   blossom honey (End of boil) ·

Fermentation

1 teaspoon (5 g) pectic enzyme

5 teaspoons (25 g) yeast nutrient

Pasteur Champagne yeast: Wyeast 4021;
   Red Star or Lalvin EC-1118; White
   Labs WLP715

Bottling

5 ounces priming sugar

Extra equipment: second pot and a food
   processor or blender

STARTING GRAVITY: 1.082

FINAL GRAVITY: 1.010

FINAL TARGET ABV: 8.5%

PROCESS

1. Add 3 gallons (11 L) of water to your brewpot.

2. As the water begins to boil, remove the pot from the heat. Add the light malt extract syrup. Stir to prevent clumping and scorching on the bottom of the pot. Return the pot to the heat.

3. Allow the wort to come up to a boil. After preboiling for 5 minutes, add the Hallertau hop pellets and stir. Start timing your 1-hour boil at the point that you make this hop addition.

4. Heat 32 ounces (950 ml) of water in a second pot to a boil, and shut off heat source. Add the dried cranberries to this water to hydrate. Stir the mixture occasionally as it cools.

5. 10 minutes before the end of the boil, add the Irish moss and stir for 1 minute. 7½ minutes before the end of the boil, purée the mixture of dried cranberries in a grain bag and water. Once this mixture is a thin paste in consistency, add it to the brewpot.

6. At the 60-minute mark, turn off heat source, and add the unfiltered orange blossom honey. Stir until all the honey is dissolved. Stir the wort clockwise for 2 minutes as you build up a whirlpool effect. Stop stirring and allow the wort to sit for 10 minutes.

7. Chill the wort in a cold water bath until it is just below 75°F (24°C).

8. Transfer the wort into a fermenter, and aerate for 1 minute. Top up to a 5-gallon (19-L) mark with water. A bucket fermenter allows easy transfer of cranberries.

9. Pitch the Pasteur Champagne yeast, pectic enzyme, and yeast nutrient into the carboy. Aerate for another minute. In about 4 weeks, your beer should be ready to package.

10. Before bottling, clean and sanitize bottles and caps and create a priming solution of 1 cup (235 ml) boiling water and priming sugar. Siphon the beer into a sterilized bottling bucket, add the water-diluted priming solution, and gently stir. Bottle and cap the braggot. Store in a warm place.

11. In another 2 weeks, your beer should be ready to drink.

PORT BARREL–AGED BELGIAN BROWN ALE

Produced for centuries in southwestern Belgium, this style of beer offers great complexity derived from wood aging, exotic fermentation, and subtle notes of fruit. An acidic mixed-yeast culture gives this beer its signature tart flavor. A healthy bit of bacteria will be incorporated into the sugar-eating process for this beer. There will be a primary fermentation on Belgian ale yeast and a secondary fermentation on a prepackaged *lactobacillus* strain. This secondary fermentation will last for about a month. During secondary fermentation, you will also add American oak chips that have been soaked in port (for both sterilizing and flavoring reasons). This process will add the final touches of complexity to this very unique and memorable beer.

INGREDIENTS

Preboil tea

4 1/2 gallons (17 L) cool water

1 1/2 pounds (700 g) Cara-pils crushed barley malt

Grain bag

2 teaspoons (10 g) gypsum

Boil

6.6 pounds (3 kg) light malt extract syrup
   (65 minutes)

  (or 5 pounds [2.3 kg] dry malt extract)

1 pound (455 g) dark Belgian candy sugar
   (65 minutes)

1 1/2 ounces (43 g) Kent Goldings hop pellets
   (60 minutes)

1/2 ounce (15 g) Saaz hop pellets *(20 minutes)*

1 teaspoon (5 g) Irish moss *(20 minutes)*

8 ounces (340 g) molasses *(10 minutes)*

Fermentation

Yeast: Wyeast 1388 or White Labs WLP570
   Belgian Strong/Golden Ale Primary

In jar during fermentation

1/4 pound (115 g) American oak chips, medium
   roast

6 ounces (175 ml) quality red port wine

Secondary fermentation

Yeast: Wyeast 5335 *Lactobacillus delbruecki*
   or White Labs WLP655 Sour Mix

Bottling

5 ounces (140 g) priming sugar

Extra equipment: quart jar to hold oak chips

STARTING GRAVITY: 1.068

FINAL GRAVITY: 1.014

FINAL TARGET ABV: 6.8%

PROCESS

1. Fill a grain bag with the crushed Cara-pils barley. Tie off the top and place the bag in your brewpot filled with $4^1/_2$ gallons (17 L) of cool water. Add the gypsum to the water. Heat the pot, and stir the water and grain bag every 5 minutes.

2. As the water reaches 170°F (77°C), pull out the specialty grain bag using a large stirring spoon. Hold the bag above the brewpot for a minute, allowing most of the liquid to drain into the pot. Do not squeeze the grain bag.

3. As the water begins to boil, remove the pot from the heat. Add the light malt extract and the dark Belgian candy sugar. Stir to prevent clumping and scorching on the bottom of the pot. Return the pot to the heat.

4. Allow the wort to come up to a boil. After preboiling for 5 minutes, add the Kent Goldings hop pellets and stir. Start timing your 1-hour boil at the point that you make this hop addition.

5. 20 minutes before the end of your boil, add the Saaz hop pellets and the Irish moss, and stir for 1 minute.

6. 10 minutes before the end of the boil, add the molasses, and stir for 1 minute.

7. At the 60-minute mark, turn off heat source. Stir the wort clockwise for 2 minutes to build up a whirlpool effect. Stop stirring and allow the wort to sit for 10 minutes.

8. Chill the wort in a cold water bath to a temperature of 70°F–75°F (21°C–24°C).

9. Transfer the wort into a carboy. Aerate for 1 minute.

10. Pitch the strong ale yeast into the carboy and aerate for another minute. Top up to the 5-gallon mark with water.

11. Place the American oak chips in a quart (900 ml) jar and pour the port over the chips. Close the jar tightly and allow it to sit at room temperature for 3 weeks or so as the beer goes through fermentation.

12. After the vigorous primary fermentation slows down (around 5 or 6 days), pitch the secondary yeast into the fermenting beer. Allow the beer to continue fermenting in a warm place (75°F [24°C]) for 2 or 3 weeks. Transfer your beer into the sterilized bottling bucket and clean and sanitize the carboy. Transfer the beer back into the carboy for the extended aging and acidification needed for this style of beer, and add the port-soaked oak chips. In about 3 or 4 months, your beer should be ready to package.

13. Before bottling, clean and sanitize the bottles and caps, and create a priming solution of 1 cup (235 ml) boiling water and priming sugar. Siphon the beer into a sterilized bottling bucket, add the water-diluted priming solution, and gently stir. Bottle and cap the beer.

14. In another 2 weeks, it should be ready to drink.

DEMA-GODDESS ALE

To make this particular recipe, you will be conducting high-gravity brewing, using several of the techniques covered earlier in this book. White or light beet sugars are more highly fermentable than barley sugars, so dose in small amounts of sugar during fermentation. However, using too much of these sugars will make a beer overly dry, cidery, and hot (boozy with no body). To reduce this effect, high-quality Demerara sugar will be added during the initial boil as well as intermittently during fermentation to keep the body of the beer up and the dryness down. With big beers, high volumes of hops need to be added just to counterbalance the sweetness that will inevitably be left via the unfermented sugars. To fully ferment this beer, two different yeast strains and a special aerating method will be used. The boiling process drives nearly all of the oxygen out of the beer as it's being made, but yeast works best in an oxygen-rich environment. Aerating your beer is therefore recommended at the start of fermentation. However, with strong beers, sometimes that isn't enough. For this beer, and all beers with a target alcohol by volume of over 12 percent, it's recommended to use an aquarium air pump, hose, and aerating stone to add high levels of oxygen just before pitching the primary yeast and just before adding the secondary yeast. This extreme aeration method can give your beer undesired, oxygenated, or cardboard flavors if done too late in the fermentation process. But stronger beers require extended periods of time to properly ferment. For primary and secondary fermentation periods lasting six to eight weeks for the combined processes, I would not recommend this method of aeration beyond the third week of total fermentation. Since you will be adding sugar repeatedly during fermentation, it will be difficult to gauge the initial and final specific gravity. However, it will be important to take hydrometer readings to measure this parameter, as you add sugars during fermentation to make sure that the yeast is still performing optimally in the alcohol-rich environment.

INGREDIENTS

Preboil tea

4 gallon (17 L) cool water

1/2 pound (225 g) crushed Cara-Munich barley

1/2 pound (225 g) crushed Special B barley

Grain bag

2 teaspoons (10 g) gypsum

Boil

13.2 pounds (6 kg) light liquid malt extract or
   11 pounds (5 kg) dry light malt extract *(65 minutes)*

2 ounces (55 g) Warrior hop pellets *(60 minutes)*

2 ounces (55 g) Chinook hop pellets *(20 minutes)*

1/2 pound (225 g) cane sugar *(20 minutes)*

2 teaspoon (10 g) Irish moss *(20 minutes)*

1/2 pound (225 g) Demerara sugar *(10 minutes)*

5 teaspoons (25 g) yeast nutrient *(After cooling)*

In carboy

Water to the 5-gallon (19-L) mark

Primary fermentation

Yeast: Wyeast 1214 Abbey Ale or White Labs
   WLP570 Belgian Strong/Golden Ale or Safbrew
   T-58

1 ounce (28 g) pure cane sugar *(Day 8)*

1 ounce (28 g) Demerara sugar *(Day 9)*

1 ounce (28 g) pure cane sugar *(Day 10)*

1 ounce (28 g) Demerara sugar *(Day 11)*

1 ounce (28 g) pure cane sugar *(Day 12)*

1 ounce (28 g) Cascade hop pellets *(Day 13)*

Distillers yeast (secondary) *(Day 13)*

1 ounce (28 g) pure cane sugar *(Day 13)*

1 ounce (28 g) Demerara sugar *(Day 14)*

1 ounce (28 g) pure cane sugar *(Day 15)*

1 ounce (28 g) Demerara sugar *(Day 16)*

1 ounce (28 g) pure cane sugar *(Day 17)*

Bottling

Champagne Yeast; Wyeast 4021; White Label WLP
   715; Red Star Champagne or Lalvin EC-1118

5 ounces (140 g) priming sugar

Extra equipment: aquarium pump/hose/aerating
   stone setup

STARTING GRAVITY: 1.100 (at the start of primary
   fermentation)

FINAL GRAVITY: With this many small sugar
   additions and this big a beer, final gravity
   is anybody's guess!

FINAL TARGET ABV: 14 to16%

Note: *Day references in the recipe above are approximations.
The day that you actually begin your postprimary fermentation
sugar additions may vary depending upon fermentation
temperatures.*

PROCESS

1. Fill a grain bag with the crushed Cara-Munich malt and the crushed Special B malt. Tie off the top and place the bag in your brewpot filled with 4 gallons (15 L) of cool water. Add the gypsum to the water. Heat the pot and stir the water and grain bag every 5 minutes.

2. As the water reaches 170°F (77°C), pull out the specialty grain bag using a large stirring spoon. Hold the bag above the brewpot for a minute, allowing most of the liquid to drain into the pot. Do not squeeze the grain bag.

3. As the water begins to boil, remove the pot from the heat. Add the light malt extract. Stir to prevent clumping and scorching on the bottom of the pot. Return to heat.

4. Allow the wort to come up to a boil. After preboiling for 5 minutes, add the Tomahawk hop pellets and stir. Start timing the 1-hour boil at the point that you make this hop addition.

5. 20 minutes before the end of the boil, add the Chinook hop pellets, 1/2 pound (225 g) of cane sugar, and the Irish moss, stir for 1 minute.

6. 10 minutes before the end of the boil. add 1/2 pound (225 g) of Demerara sugar. and stir for 1 minute.

7. At the 60-minute mark of the boil, turn off the heat source. Stir the wort clockwise for 2 minutes as you build up a whirlpool effect. Stop stirring and allow the wort to sit for 10 minutes.

8. Chill the wort in a cold water bath to a temperature of 70°F–75°F (21°C–24°C).

9. Transfer the wort into a carboy. Add the yeast nutrient.

10. Pitch the primary strong ale yeast into carboy. Top up the wort to the 5-gallon (19-L) mark with water. Set up the aquarium pump, hose, and aeration stone, and oxygenate beer for 1 hour.

11. After the vigorous primary fermentation slows down (around 8 to 10 days), you will hear the airlock bubbling less frequently. Once this slowdown occurs, alternate between 1 ounce (28 g) of pure cane sugar and 1 ounce (28 g) of Demerara sugar additions to the carboy every day for 5 days straight.

12. A few days after the primary fermentation slows down, transfer your beer into the sterilized bottling bucket while you clean out the carboy. Many yeast cells have grown in this sugar-rich environment, and you want to leave the layer of dead/dormant yeast cells that have dropped to the bottom of the carboy behind as you transfer to the bottling bucket.

13. Add the Cascade hop pellets to the empty, sterilized carboy. Transfer the beer back into your sterilized carboy and pitch your secondary super high-gravity yeast. A yeast starter is a good idea. (See Resources, page 217.) Set up your aquarium pump/hose/aerating stone unit once again and aerate the beer for 1 full hour. Again, you will be adding 1 ounce (28 g) of pure cane sugar followed by 1 ounce (28 g) of Demerara sugar the next day for 5 straight days. The difference here is that you begin the sugar additions the day that you transfer and aerate the beer for secondary fermentation. Secondary fermentation should last 1 to 3 weeks. 2 weeks after all fermentation activity subsides, your beer should be ready to package.

14. For this high-gravity beer, you will be adding additional yeast at bottling to make sure that the beer has fresh yeast for the bottle conditioning. While transferring the beer to the bottling bucket, use a cup of the beer to dissolve the Champagne yeast. Add the Champagne yeast mixture to the bottling bucket and stir well. Now add the priming sugar dissolved in 1 cup (235 ml) boiling water to the bottling bucket, and stir well before bottling.

15. In another 4–6 weeks, your beer should be ready to drink. Due to its higher alcohol content, this beer is slow to carbonate. This is another long keeper, and will mature well with age. It will be better after a year of aging, if you can wait that long.

E-Brew

Extreme Beer Wars: My brewery, Dogfish Head, and the Boston Beer Company have passed the belt back and forth several times over as Brewer of the world's strongest beer. Boston Beer now has the title but Dogfish Head brews more styles and more volume of 15 percent ABV beers than any brewery in the world.

CHAPTER 9

Master Brewers' Recipes

IN THE BOOK *GREAT BEERS* of Belgium (Media Marketing Communications, 2003), world-renowned beer authority Michael Jackson wrote of Belgium, "No country has given birth to so many different styles of beer... no country has so many individualistic, idiosyncratic beers." I recently arranged a trip to Belgium to visit the legendary birthplace of craft brewing with four of the industry's highly-respected craft brewers: Adam Avery of Avery Brewing Company, Boulder, Colorado; Rob Tod of Allagash Brewing Company, Portland, Maine; Tomme Arthur of Port Brewing Company, San Diego, California; Vinnie Cilurzo of Russian River Brewery, San Francisco, California; yours truly; and our fearless leader, Lorenzo "Kuaska" DaBova. In this book, each of these innovative brewers has agreed to share one of his secret recipes with aspiring homebrewers. In addition, two of Dogfish Head's esteemed brewers, Bryan Selders and Mike Gerhart, have contributed Dogfish Head beer recipes to this chapter as well. Both Mike and Bryan approach their work with the perspective and focus of true artists. They are capable of taking the ideas and theories that we come up with for pushing the boundaries on what a beer can be and turning the hypothetical into the actual: a beautiful, iconoclastic pint of beer.

T'EJ

INGREDIENTS

Preboil

6 gallons (23 L) water

Beginning of boil

3.3 pounds (1.5 kg) light liquid malt extract

  (or 2.5 pounds [1 kg] dry malt extract)

8 pounds (3.6 kg) honey

Fermentation

Yeast: Wyeast 4632 Dry Mead or Wyeast 4184 Sweet Mead; or White Labs WLP 720 Sweet Mead Yeast or Dry Champagne

9.6 ounces (272 g) Gesho (a tree root native to Africa) *(Day 3)*

Grain bag *(Day 3)*

Bottling

5 ounces (140 g) priming sugar

STARTING GRAVITY: 1.080

FINAL GRAVITY: 1.014

FINAL TARGET ABV: 9.5 to 10%

Mike Gerhart, Dogfish Head Craft Brewery

T'ej (pronounced "Ted-j") is an Ethiopian honey wine that is as popular today as it was over 100 years ago. This version is a slight variation to the traditional style with the addition of barley malt. The bittering agent is ground, or shredded Gesho tree root, available through African specialty food suppliers, or see Extreme Brewing Company in the Resource section, page 217. This unique and flavorful beverage is an excellent accompaniment to spicy food and good conversation. So find an Ethiopian cookbook, gather some good friends, and raise a glass! As they say in Ethiopia, "T'chen Chen!"

PROCESS

1. In a brew kettle, heat 6 gallons (23 L) of water to a boil. Remove from heat and add malt extract and honey. Return to a boil.

2. Boil to 5½ (21 L) gallons.

3. Cool to 75°F (24°C).

4. Rack to a fermenter and pitch with mead yeast.

5. Allow to ferment for 3 days.

6. Remove 2.4 gallons (9 L), and place in a separate pot. Place the Gesho in a grain bag, add it to the pot, and bring the liquid to a boil. Simmer for 15 minutes.

7. Remove Gesho, and then cool to 75°F (24°C).

8. Return this portion to the fermenter and allow fermentation to continue to completion.

9. Rack to secondary fermenter and allow 14 more days of cool conditioning.

10. Before bottling, clean and sanitize bottles and caps and create a priming solution of 1 cup (235 ml) boiling water and priming sugar. Siphon beer into a sterilized bottling bucket, add the water-diluted priming solution, and gently stir. Bottle and cap beer. Beer will be ready to drink in about 2 weeks.

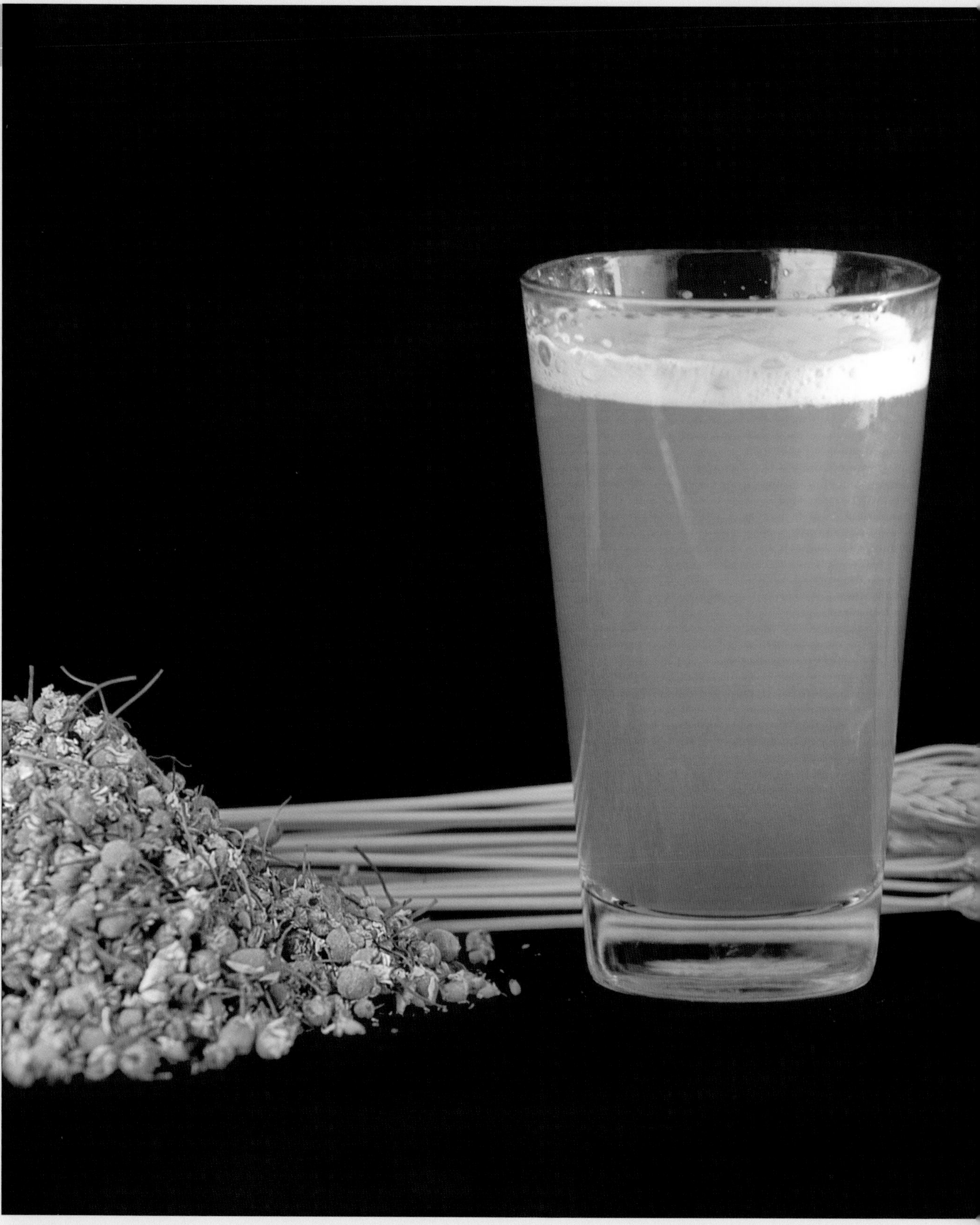

WILDFLOWER WHEAT

Mike Gerhart, Dogfish Head Craft Brewery

The addition of chamomile flowers and honey lends this American style wheat beer a soothing character that complements warm weather and relaxation. This brew was originally made in the summer of 2005 at Dogfish Head Brewery & Eats in Rehoboth Beach, Delaware, where it was a huge success.

PROCESS

1. In a brew kettle, heat 6 gallons (23 L) of water to a boil. Remove from heat and add malt extract and honey. Return to a boil.

2. Place chamomile flowers into a mesh sack and seal. After 15 minutes, add Vanguard hops and chamomile to the kettle. Boil for 60 minutes.

3. Remove from heat and swirl the contents of the kettle to create a whirlpool.

4. Cool the wort and rack to a fermenter leaving as much of the solids behind in the kettle as possible. (It's okay to get some of the sediment into the fermenter as it is beneficial to yeast health.)

5. Pitch the cooled wort with American wheat yeast and ferment at around 68°F to 71°F (20°C–22°C). Allow to sit for 24 hours after fermentation is complete.

6. Cool and rack to secondary fermenter and allow 5 more days of conditioning.

7. Before bottling, clean and sanitize bottles and caps and create a priming solution of 1 cup (235 ml) boiling water and priming sugar. Siphon beer into a sterilized bottling bucket, add the water-diluted priming solution, and gently stir. Bottle and cap beer. Beer will be ready to drink in about 2 weeks.

INGREDIENTS

Preboil tea

6 gallons (23 L) water

Boil

6.6 pounds (3 kg) wheat/barley liquid malt extract *(75 minutes)*

(or 5 pounds [2.3 kg] wheat/barley dry malt extract)

1 pound (455 g) honey *(75 minutes)*

1 ounce (28 g) Vanguard hops *(60 minutes)*

Grain bag *(60 minutes)*

2 ounces (55 g) whole chamomile flowers *(60 minutes)*

Fermentation

American wheat yeast: White Lab WLP320 or Wyeast 1010 or Safebrew WB-06

Bottling

5 ounces (140 g) priming sugar

STARTING GRAVITY: 1.057

FINAL GRAVITY: 1.008

FINAL TARGET ABV: 5.5%

IBUS: 15

IMPERIAL STOUT

INGREDIENTS

Mash

4½ gallons (17 L) water

2 grain bags

Steep at 155°F (68°C)

6 ounces (75 g) Dingemans Cara 8 (caramel-pils) malt, crushed

5 ounces (63 g) Dingemans Debittered Black malt, crushed

5 ounces (63 g) Dingemans Chocolate malt, crushed

5 ounces (63 g) Weyerman Dehusked Carafa III malt, crushed

12 ounces (150 g) Gambrinus honey malt, crushed

12 ounces (150 g) Dingemans Cara 45 malt, crushed

Preboil

12 pounds (5.4 kg) dry dark malt extract

Boil

¾ pound (340 g) Turbinado or brown sugar (60 minutes)

½ ounces (15 g) Magnum hops *(60 minutes)*

½ ounces (15 g) Magnum hops *(30 minutes)*

1½ ounces (35 g) Sterling hops *(End of boil)*

Fermentation

Yeast: Wyeast 1056 or White Labs WLP001 ale yeast or Safale US-05

Bottling

5 ounces (140 g) priming sugar

STARTING GRAVITY: 1.104

FINAL GRAVITY: 1.024

FINAL TARGET ABV: 10.7%

IBUs: 46

Adam Avery, Avery Brewing Company

This is a souped–up interpretation on a traditional beer that has been brewed in Europe for centuries. An early example in the American craft brewing renaissance was brewed by Grant's Brewery in Washington state.

PROCESS

1. Steep the crushed Dingemans Cara 8, Dingemans Debittered Black, Dingemans Chocolate, Weyermans Dehusked Caraf, Gambrinus honey malt and Dingemans Cara 45 malt at 155°F (68°C) in 4½ gallons (17 L) of water for 30 minutes in 2 grain bags.

2. Remove crushed grains and add the dark malt extract and the Turbinado. Stir well. Bring to a boil.

3. Add ½ ounce (21 g) of the Magnum hops and boil for 30 minutes.

4. Add the remaining ½ ounce (15 g) of Magnum hops and boil for 30 more minutes.

5. Remove from heat and add 1½ ounces (35 g) Sterling hops.

6. Cool to 70°F (21°C), oxygenate, and rack to fermenter adding the necessary cold water to achieve gravity of 1.104.

7. Pitch yeast ferment at 70°F (21°C).

8. When fermentation is complete, rack to secondary vessel for 4 weeks.

9. Before bottling, clean and sanitize bottles and caps and create a priming solution of 1 cup (235 ml) boiling water and priming sugar. Siphon beer into a sterilized bottling bucket, add the water-diluted priming solution, and gently stir. Bottle and cap beer. Beer will be ready to drink in about 2 weeks.

BELGIAN WIT

Rob Tod, Allagash Brewing Company

This is a traditional Belgian-style wit that can be enjoyed all year. It's very refreshing served ice cold in the summer, and during the cooler seasons it can be served at cellar temperatures where it will nicely express a subtle spice character. Wits are traditionally spiced; in addition to orange peels, this recipe calls for coriander freshly crushed from whole seeds just before the brew. When making this, try experimenting by adding your own "secret spice." Some suggestions for spices are: anise, cinnamon, vanilla, pepper, or ginger. Just use a tiny pinch. Character added by the spice should only be a barely identifiable note in the background.

The key to the proper flavor profile (and a nice complement to the spices) is the use of a traditional Belgian wit yeast. Most commercial yeast suppliers have yeast strains specifically designed for Belgian wits. Or, if you're feeling adventurous, you can try culturing some yeast from a bottle. Many commercial producers of these beers don't filter out the yeast, and a healthy yeast culture often rests at the bottom of a fresh bottle.

INGREDIENTS

Preboil

6 gallons (23 L) water

Boil

6.6 pounds (3 kg) 40% wheat/60% barley liquid malt extract (or 5 pounds [2.3 kg] wheat/barley dry malt extract) *(75 minutes)*

3/4 ounce (21 g) Tettnanger hops (bittering) *(60 minutes)*

3/4 ounces (21 g) Saaz hops (flavor) *(30 minutes)*

1/4 ounce (7 g) Saaz hops (aroma) *(End of boil)*

1/4 ounce (7 g) freshly crushed coriander *(End of boil)*

1/4 ounce (7 g) bitter orange peel *(End of boil)*

1 pinch "secret spice" *(End of boil)*

Fermentation

Belgian wit yeast: White Labs WLP400 Belgian Wit Ale or WLP410 Belgian Wit II; or Wyeast 3944 Belgian Wit beer or 3463 Forbidden Fruit Yeast or Safbrew T-58

Bottling

5 ounces (140 g) priming sugar

STARTING GRAVITY: 1.048
FINAL GRAVITY: 1.010
FINAL TARGET ABV: 4.8 percent
IBUS: 18

PROCESS

1. In a brew kettle, heat 6 gallons (23 L) of water to a boil. Remove from heat and add malt extract. Return to a boil.

2. After 15 minutes, add Tettnanger bittering hops.

3. Boil for 30 minutes.

4. Add first Saaz (flavor) hops and boil for 30 minutes.

5. At end of boil, add second Saaz aroma hops, coriander, orange peel, and a pinch of a "secret spice."

6. Remove from heat, swirl contents of kettle to create whirlpool, and allow to rest for 15 minutes.

7. Cool wort and rack to fermenter leaving as many of the solids behind in the kettle as possible.

8. Pitch cooled wort with Belgian wit yeast, and ferment at 70°F (21°C) until fermentation is complete.

9. Before bottling, clean and sanitize bottles and caps and create a priming solution of 1 cup (235 ml) boiling water and priming sugar. Siphon beer into a sterilized bottling bucket, add the water-diluted priming solution, and gently stir. Bottle and cap beer. Beer will be ready to drink in about 2 weeks.

60-MINUTE IPA

INGREDIENTS

Pre-boil tea at 150°F (66°C)

6 gallons (23 L) water

Grain bag

6 ounces (175 g) crushed amber malt

Boil

7 pounds (3.2 kg) light dry malt extract
(75 minutes)

1/2 ounce (15 g) Warrior hops
(Add gradually over 60 minutes)

1/2 ounce (15 g) Simcoe hops
(Add gradually over 60 minutes)

1/2 ounces (15 g) Amarillo hops
(Add gradually over 60 minutes)

1 teaspoon (5 g) Irish moss

1/2 ounces (15 g) Amarillo hops
(End of boil)

Fermentation

Yeast: Wyeast 1187 Ringwood Ale or
   Safale S-04; or White Labs WLP 005

1 ounce (28 g) Amarillo hops
(6 to 7 days)

1/2 ounce (15 g) Simcoe hops
(6 to 7 days)

Bottling

5 ounces (140 g) priming sugar

STARTING GRAVITY: 1.064

FINAL GRAVITY: 1.017

FINAL TARGET ABV: 6%

IBUs: 60

Bryan Selders, Dogfish Head Craft Brewery

This is a DIY version of Dogfish Head's best-selling beer. This beer uses a unique method called continual hopping. Traditionally, beers are brewed with two major hop additions: one early in the boil for bitterness and one at the end of the boil for aroma. We asked ourselves: "What would happen if we add a series of minor hop additions that occur evenly throughout the length of the boil?" From this, the idea of continual hopping was born. This recipe calls for adding the small doses of hops by hand but you may also make your own continual-hopping device.

PROCESS

1. In a brew kettle, heat 6 gallons (23 L) of water to 150°F (66°C). In a grain bag, add the crushed British amber malt. Allow to steep for 15 minutes.

2. Remove the grain bag and bring water to a boil. While waiting for a boil, blend together the Warrior hops with 1/2 (15 g) ounce of Simcoe and 1/2 ounce (15 g) of Amarillo hops.

3. Remove from heat and add the light malt extract.

4. Return to a boil.

5. After 15 minutes, begin adding the hop blend a little at a time so it takes 60 minutes to add all of the hops to the kettle.

6. After 60 minutes, remove the kettle from the heat and stir the wort to create a whirlpool while adding another 1/2 ounce (15 g) of Amarillo hops to the liquid. Cover and allow to settle for 20 minutes.

7. Cool the wort and rack to a fermenter, leaving as many of the solids behind in the kettle as possible. (It's okay to get some of the sediment into the fermenter as it's beneficial to yeast health.)

8. Pitch the cooled wort with ale yeast and ferment at around 68°F–71°F (20°C–22°C). "Rock the baby" to aerate the wort.

9. After 6 to 7 days, rack the beer to the secondary fermenter leaving behind as much yeast and trub as possible and add 1 (28 g) ounce of Amarillo hops and 1/2 ounce (15 g) of Simcoe hops.

10. Allow beer to condition in a secondary fermenter for 12 to 14 days.

11. Before bottling, clean and sanitize bottles and caps and create a priming solution of 1 cup (235 ml) boiling water and priming sugar. Siphon beer into a sterilized bottling bucket, add the water-diluted priming solution, and gently stir. Note: A hop bag, or some type of coarse clothing over the end of the racking cane will help prevent it from getting stopped up by the hops from dry hopping. Bottle and cap beer. Beer will be ready to drink in about 2 weeks.

The Zopinator

*Paul Zocco,
Zok's Homebrewing
Supplies*

A FEW YEARS AGO, Dogfish Head Craft Brewery started producing some unusual IPAs, barley wines and other over-the-top beers using a continuous hopping device they created called Sir Hops Alot. Being an avid homebrewer, I wanted to brew beers like these guys were making: big, hoppy beers full of too much of everything, especially hops. Being somewhat of a gadget-type person, I also wanted to build and use a continuous hop feeder, similar to the hopper at Dogfish Head. What I envisioned was a device that would drop a steady stream of hop pellets into my boiling kettle throughout the entire boil. Leaf or hop plugs would probably work, but ultimately, my gadget was meant for use with hop pellets. Of the three hop types, hop pellets seemed to be the most consistent in shape and I thought they would be the easiest to design around. My home-scale version of Sir Hops Alot, the Zopinator, is much smaller, made from easily obtained components and everyday tools, and is affordable for the average homebrewer. Instructions to make the Zopinator can be found online at www.dogfish.com.

INDIAN BROWN ALE

INGREDIENTS

Pre-boil tea at 150° F (66° C)

6 gallons (23 L) water

Grain bag

10 ounces (280 g) crushed British amber malt

10 ounces (280 g) crushed 60 Lovibond crystal malt

8 ounces (225 g) crushed light chocolate malt

2 ounces (55 g) crushed roasted barley

Boil

7 pounds (3.2 kg) light dry malt extract *(75 minutes)*

1/2 ounce (15 g) Warrior hops *(60 minutes)*

8 ounces (225 g) dark brown sugar *(10 minutes)*

1 ounce (28 g) Vanguard hops *(End of boil)*

Fermentation

Yeast: Ringwood ale yeast/Wyeast 1187 or Safale S-04 dry or White Labs WLP 005

Bottling

5 ounces (140 g) priming sugar

STARTING GRAVITY: 1.070

FINAL GRAVITY: 1.015

FINAL TARGET ABV: 7.2%

IBUs: 50

Bryan Selders, Dogfish Head Craft Brewery

This is a stealth beer and its higher alcohol levels are well masked by a fair amount of body. Indian Brown Ale has the color of an American brown ale, the hopping rate of an IPA, and the caramel sweetness of a Scotch ale.

PROCESS

1. In a brew kettle, heat 6 gallons (23 L) of water to 150°F (66°C). In a grain bag, add all 4 of the crushed grains. Allow to steep for 15 minutes.

2. Remove the grain bag and bring water to a boil.

3. Remove from heat and add the light malt extract.

4. Return to a boil.

5. After 15 minutes, add the Warrior hops to the kettle and continue to boil for and additional 60 minutes.

6. 10 minutes before the end of the boil, add the dark brown sugar, stirring until the sugar dissolves completely.

7. At the end of the boil, add the Vanguard hops, remove the kettle from the heat; stir to create a whirlpool, cover and let it settle for 20 minutes.

8. Cool the wort and rack to a fermenter leaving as many of the solids behind in the kettle as possible. (It's okay to get some of the sediment into the fermenter as it is beneficial to yeast health.)

9. Pitch the cooled wort with the Ringwood ale yeast and ferment at around 68°F–71°F (20°C–22°C). Aerate the wort.

10. After 7 to 10 days, rack the beer to the secondary fermenter and allow beer to condition in secondary for 14 to 20 days.

11. Before bottling, clean and sanitize bottles and caps and create a priming solution of 1 cup (235 ml) boiling water and priming sugar. Siphon beer into a sterilized bottling bucket, add the water-diluted priming solution, and gently stir. Bottle and cap beer. Beer will be ready to drink in about 2 weeks.

RAISON D'ETRE

Bryan Selders, Dogfish Head Craft Brewery

This is one of the earliest recipes we successfully produced at our brewpub in Rehoboth Beach. The raisins give it a lot of red wine character and the Belgian yeast and beet sugars add to its complexity. This beer was designed backwards from the idea of creating a beverage that would serve as the ultimate complement to a steak dinner.

INGREDIENTS

Pre-boil tea at 150°F (66°C)

6 gallons (23 L) water

Grain bag

4 ounces (50 g) crushed 60 Lovibond crystal malt

8 ounces (100 g) crushed light chocolate malt

Boil

8 pounds (3.6 kg) light dry malt extract *(75 minutes)*

¼ ounce (7 g) Warrior hops *(60 minutes)*

2 cups hot wort from brewpot *(10 minutes)*

6 ounces (170 g) puréed raisins *(10 minutes)*

8 ounces (225 g) Belgian candi sugar *(10 minutes)*

½ ounce (15 g) Vanguard hops *(End of boil)*

Fermentation

Yeast: Wyeast 3522 Belgian ale, White Labs WLP545 or WLP550 or Safbrew T-58

Bottling

5 ounces (140 g) priming sugar

STARTING GRAVITY: 1.078

FINAL GRAVITY: 1.016

FINAL TARGET ABV: 8%

IBUs: 25

PROCESS

1. In a brew kettle, heat 6 gallons (23 L) of water to 150°F (66°C). In a grain bag, add the crushed crystal and chocolate malts. Allow to steep for 15 minutes.

2. Remove the grain bag and bring water to a boil. While waiting for a boil, combine raisins with 2 cups (475 ml) of liquid from the kettle in a blender and purée until smooth.

3. Remove from heat and add the light malt extract.

4. Return to a boil.

5. After 15 minutes, add the Warrior hops to the kettle and continue to boil for and additional 60 minutes.

6. 10 minutes before the end of the boil, add the raisins and candi sugar, stirring until the sugar dissolves completely.

7. At the end of the boil, add the Vanguard hops. Remove the kettle from the heat, stir to create a whirlpool, cover, and let it settle for 20 minutes.

8. Cool the wort and rack to a fermenter leaving as many of the solids behind in the kettle as possible. (It's okay to get some of the sediment into the fermenter as it is beneficial to yeast health.)

9. Pitch the cooled wort with the Belgian ale yeast and ferment at around 71°F–74°F (22°C–23°C). "Rock the baby" to aerate the wort.

10. After 7 to 10 days, rack the beer to the secondary fermenter and allow beer to condition in secondary for 14 to 20 days.

11. Before bottling, clean and sanitize bottles and caps and create a priming solution of 1 cup (235 ml) boiling water and priming sugar. Siphon beer into a sterilized bottling bucket, add the water-diluted priming solution, and gently stir. Bottle and cap beer. Beer will be ready to drink in about 2 weeks.

MIDAS TOUCH

Bryan Selders, Dogfish Head Craft Brewery

The recipe for Midas Touch was discovered in a 2,700-year-old tomb in Turkey, believed to belong to King Midas. In addition to its exotic pedigree, the saffron, honey, white Muscat grapes, and higher-than-average alcohol content are what make this recipe so special.

PROCESS

1. In a brew kettle, heat 6 gallons (23 L) of water to a boil. Remove from heat and add light malt extract and honey. Return to a boil.

2. After 15 minutes, add Simcoe hops. Boil for 60 minutes.

3. Remove from heat and add saffron threads and swirl contents of kettle to create a whirlpool.

4. Cool the wort and rack to a fermenter leaving as much of the solids behind in the kettle as possible. (It's okay to get some of the sediment into the fermenter as it is beneficial to yeast health.)

5. Pitch the cooled wort with a fairly neutral ale yeast and ferment at around 68°F to 71°F (20°C–22°C). "Rock the baby" to aerate the wort.

6. After the most vigorous fermentation subsides (about 3 days), add the White Muscat grape juice concentrate. Rock the baby again.

7. Ferment for 5 to 7 more days then rack to secondary fermenter. Allow beer to condition for 12 to 14 days.

INGREDIENTS

Preboil

6 gallons (23 L) water

Boil

8 pounds (3.6 kg) light liquid malt extract *(75 minutes)* (or 5.5 pounds [2.5 kg] light dry malt extract)

2 pounds (900 g) clover honey *(75 minutes)*

1/4 ounce (7 g) Simcoe hops *(60 minutes)*

10 Saffron threads *(End of boil)*

Fermentation

White Labs WLP001 or Wyeast 1056 ale yeast or Safale US-05

1 quart (1 L) White Muscat grape juice concentrate *(3 days)*

Bottling

5 ounces (140 g) priming sugar

STARTING GRAVITY: 1.086

FINAL GRAVITY: 1.026

FINAL TARGET ABV: 9%

IBUS: 12

8. Before bottling, clean and sanitize bottles and caps and create a priming solution of 1 cup (235 ml) boiling water and priming sugar. Siphon beer into a sterilized bottling bucket, add the water-diluted priming solution, and gently stir. Bottle and cap beer. Beer will be ready to drink in about 2 weeks.

MO BETTA BRETTA

Tomme Arthur, Port Brewing Company

The recipe for Mo Betta Bretta was a collaborative effort between Tomme Arthur and Peter Bouckaert of New Belgium Brewing Co. The beer was fermented with 100 percent *Brettanomyces anomoalus*. It is believed to be the first beer brewed and sold in the United States that was solely made with *Brettanomyces*.

PROCESS

1. In a brew kettle, heat 6 gallons (23 L) of water to a 170°F (77°C). Remove from heat and add light malt extract, flaked oats, German Munich malt, and Cara-pils, steeping them for 15 minutes. Remove grain sack and bring the mixture to a boil.

2. After 15 minutes, add German Magnum hops. Boil for 60 minutes.

3. Remove from heat. After 5 minutes, swirl contents in kettle to create a whirlpool.

4. Cool the wort and rack to a fermenter leaving as much of the solids behind in the kettle as possible. (It's okay to get some of the sediment into the fermenter as it is beneficial to yeast health.)

5. Pitch the cooled wort with 1 quart (946 ml) culture of *Brettanomyces Anomoalus*. Fermentation should begin in less than 24 hours at around 68°F to 71°F (20°C–22°C). Shake the fermenter vigorously for 3 to 5 minutes.

6. Fermentation will take between 14 to 21 days depending on the size of the yeast culture.

INGREDIENTS

Pre-boil tea

6 gallons (23 L) water

7 pounds (3 kg) light malt extract

3/4 pounds (340 g) flaked oats

3/4 pounds (340 g) Munich malt

3/4 pounds (340 g) Cara-pils malt

Boil

1/4 ounce (7 g) Magnum hops
    (60 minutes)

Fermentation

White Labs WLP645

Bottling

5 ounces (140 g) priming sugar

STARTING GRAVITY: 1.060

FINAL GRAVITY: 1.008

FINAL TARGET ABV: 6.8%

IBUs: 18

7. After primary fermentation, allow 7 to 14 more days to ensure that the beer has reached terminal gravity. Brett cultures are capable of lengthy fermentations.

8. Rack to secondary fermenter. Allow beer to condition for 12 to 14 days.

9. Before bottling, clean and sanitize bottles and caps and create a priming solution of 1 cup (235 ml) boiling water and priming sugar. Siphon beer into a sterilized bottling bucket, add the water-diluted priming solution, and gently stir. Bottle and cap beer. Beer will be ready to drink in about 2 weeks.

HOPFATHER DOUBLE IPA

INGREDIENTS

Heat to 150° F (66°C)

6 gallons (233 L)

Pre-boil tea

1 pound (0.5 kg) cracked crystal 15–20 Lovibond malt *(15 minutes)*

Boil

10 pounds (3 kg) light dry malt extract *(90 minutes)*

1 ounce (28 g) Magnum hops *(90 minutes)*

1 1/2 ounces (43 g) Columbus hops *(90 minutes)*

1 1/2 ounces (43 g) Columbus hops *(30 minutes)*

3 1/2 ounces (100 g) Columbus hops *(End of boil)*

1 1/2 ounces (43 g) Willamette hops *(End of boil)*

Fermentation

Yeast: White LabsWLP001 California Ale or Safale US-05 Yeast or Wyeast Chico 1056 Ale Yeast

1/2 ounces (15 g) Columbus hops *(Day 3 to 5)*

1/4 ounce (7 g) Chinook hops *(Day 3 to 5)*

1/4 ounce (7 g) Amarillo hops *(Day 3 to 5)*

3/4 ounce (21 g) Chinook hops *(Day 7)*

Bottling

5 ounces (140 g) priming sugar

STARTING GRAVITY: 1.066 to 1.069

FINAL GRAVITY: 1.012 to 1.014

FINAL TARGET ABV: 7 to 7.5%

IBUS: 100

Vinnie Cilurzo, Russian River Brewing Company

PROCESS

1. In a brew kettle, heat 6 gallons (23 L) of water to 150°F (66°C).

2. Place cracked crystal malt in a mesh steeping bag and place in kettle. Let steep for 15 minutes.

3. Remove the mesh bag and bring the wort to a boil.

4. Once boiling, turn off heat and add light dry malt extract, 1 ounce (28 g) of Magnum hops, and 1 1/2 ounces (43 g) of the Columbus hops and return to a boil. Boil for 90 minutes.

5. Add 1 1/2 ounces (50 g) of Columbus hops and boil for 30 minutes.

6. Add 3 1/2 ounces (100 g) Columbus hops and 1 1/2 ounces (43 g) Willamette hops and turn off the heat.

7. Swirl contents of kettle to create a whirlpool.

8. Cool the wort and rack to a fermenter leaving as many of the solids behind in the kettle as possible.

9. Pitch the cooled wort with the ale yeast at 68°F (20°C).

10. Add air through a carbonating stone or rock the fermenter gently to get air mixed in with wort and yeast and ferment for five to seven days.

11. Once the fermentation is complete, add 1/2 ounce (15 g) of Columbus hops, 1/4 ounce (7 g) Amarillo hops, and 1/4 ounce (7 g) Chinook hops to fermenter.

12. After 7 days, rack beer to a secondary fermenter and add 3/4 ounce (21 g) Chinook hops and let sit for 3 to 5 more days.

13. Before bottling, clean and sanitize bottles and caps and create a priming solution of 1 cup (235 ml) boiling water and priming sugar. Siphon beer into a sterilized bottling bucket, add the water-diluted priming solution, and gently stir. Bottle and cap beer. Beer will be ready to drink in about 2 weeks.

Wild Beers

Tomme Arthur, Port Brewing Company

The beer known as lambic comes in many forms. Yet in every form, it is an aged product. Some cafés serve "young lambic" that has been aged less than one year. When it is served as "straight lambic," it has been aged more than one year and is served as a "still" or noncarbonated beer. Oftentimes, it's sweetened and served as "Faro." The two most common forms of lambic are gueze and fruited. Gueze is a blend of old and young lambic; the blending of the two beers provides a sugar source and produces a finished lambic that is highly carbonated and incredibly refreshing. Every lambic producer broadens his or her range of lambic beers through the addition of fruit with *kriek* (cherry), *framboise* (raspberry), and *peche* (peach) being the most common.

Homebrewing Lambic Beers

Typically, lambic beers are fermented from a mix of microorganisms that are present in the air at commercial breweries. The wort is inoculated overnight in a coolship (a very shallow but large open-top tank) where the wort chills in the cool night air. All the necessary organisms, including the two most important ones, *Peddiococcus* and *Brettanomyces*, are present in this airborne mixture.

To reproduce these results at home requires patience, some special equipment, and the willingness to throw caution to the wind. For the adventurous brewers looking to try something completely new, these beers represent a departure from the everyday brewing process. We refer to this as the proverbial fork in the road. It requires a leap of faith coupled with a willingness to commit to a process, which invariably has mixed results.

Microorganisms

In order to make lambic style beers at home, you need to first obtain the cultures for the fermentation. These cultures are both readily available from White Labs and Wyeast. Each has their own blend of cultures that they make available to professional, as well as homebrewers. However, many yeast ranchers prefer to culture the dregs from the bottom of lambic beers. This can be an excellent source of microorganisms. It also can be very rewarding as you can "taste" your way to the bottom of the bottle, with each sip yielding a better appreciation of the flavors you will be developing in your beer. Because many of the microorganisms can be quite invasive, it's important to maintain some separate pieces of equipment for the fermentation and transferring of these beers. If you use White Labs or Wyeast, I suggest following their directions as each company has a research and development department that provides guidelines for the lambic cultures they sell. Creating your lambic beers from malt extract is the simplest way to make great tasting lambics at home.

Mo Betta Bretta

The malt extract used in this recipe contains more dextrins than an all-grain mash, which makes it a good source for brewing lambic at home. The one drawback of using malt extract is that it tends to be darker in color (the result of the extracting process) and lambic-styled beers made at home often are slightly darker in color than traditional lambic.

The homebrewer wishing to make lambics at home would be better served to add a traditional ale yeast to convert the bulk of the sugars into alcohol. A less attenuated strain helps in this situation as the microorganisms need a source of fuel for the long journey that awaits them. After primary fermentation, the beer will be racked to a secondary fermenter. You will also add the dregs from the two bottles of lambic that you have consumed and let the yeast and microorganisms do their work. After about six weeks, a layer of scum known as a pellicle should form. This is a protective layer that keeps oxygen from rapidly infusing itself in the beer. Too much oxygen getting in equals too much acetic acid production, which means you have just made 5 gallons (19 L) of vinegar or balsamic salad dressing. I like a nice spring mix but 5 gallons (19 L) of salad dressing is just too much.

During the first six months in the secondary fermenter, the *Peddiococcus* will get to work producing a definitive sourness in the beer. When the Pedio has completed its job, the *Brettanomyces* (a wild yeast) will get busy and start making all sorts of interesting aroma compounds as it finishes out the fermentation of the remaining sugars. These flavors are often described as barnyard, feral, and musty and are the signature of a great lambic beer.

After about one year, the beer should be ready to be packaged. A unique beer like this would most definitely benefit from spending more time aging in a bottle. Traditionally, lambics are bottled in 375 ml or 750 ml Champagne bottles. Doing this allows many bottles to be aged in "caveus" for extended periods before being released. The homebrewer who is successful in recreating a lambic beer should keep sufficient stock around to open on special occasions and having bottles makes this much easier.

After the yeast has worked its magic and fermentation is complete, it's time to transfer the beer so that it can be packaged. Since the production of CO_2 is a natural byproduct of the fermentation process, both homebrewers and commercial brewers capture this CO_2 to carbonate their beers. Most homebrewers bottle-condition their beers by dosing them with a small amount of priming (corn) sugar or powdered barley malt. The priming sugar is put into the bucket or carboy just before bottling. Once in the sealed bottle, this new sugar source reinvigorates the yeast cells that were dormant and the beer referments. In this closed environment, the CO_2 that is produced has nowhere to go so it is absorbed by the beer thus naturally carbonating it. Once the beer is carbonated, it's ready to be chilled, opened, and enjoyed.

CHAPTER 10

Deluxe Brews

HERE IS YOUR CHANCE to take your brewing to the outer edges. You can use the contributors' recipes to reproduce some of the most remarkable extreme brews available today, or be inspired by their avant-garde brewing and unlikely ingredient pairings to take your homebrews in a completely new direction. The first beer in the chapter, Josh Campbell's Turkey Drool, features step-by-step photos that will help walk you through the beer-making process. From there, you'll experience a dizzying amount of subtle sweetness and the punch-in-the-taste-buds goodness of toasty malts and savory herbs and spices. It's a collection of craft brews unlike any other, and it should be all you need to get your imagination running wild.

TURKEY DROOL

Josh Campbell, Xtreme Brewing

This tawny copper-amber brew builds a major drool factor first with the sultry dark cherry aroma of the mahlab (Turkish cherry pits) and earthy notes of toffee, then with the complex flavors of cherry, raisin, caramel and the earthy notes of the Mexican herb, Epazote, kicked with rock candy sugar combined with a hint of vanilla and the richness of 6 different malts. Taste Turkey Drool once and be a fan forever.

INGREDIENTS

Preboil tea

6 gallons (23 L) water

5 gallons (19 L) cool water

8 ounces (230 g) honey malt, crushed

8 ounces (230 g) rye malt, crushed

8 ounces (230 g) Special B malt, crushed

4 ounces (115 g) Black Patent malt, crushed

2 grain bags

Boil

¼ ounce (7 g) Magnum hops *(60 minutes)*

3 pounds (1.4 kg) light dry malt extract
(65 minutes)

3 pounds (1.4 kg) wheat dry malt extract
(65 minutes)

½ ounce (14 g) Perle pellet hops (bittering)
(60 minutes)

1 teaspoon (5 g) Irish moss *(20 minutes)*

14 ounces (400 g) rock sugar *(20 minutes)*

½ ounce (14 g) Hallertau pellet hops
(15 minutes)

½ ounce (14 g) Mahlab seed, crushed
(End of boil)

½ teaspoon Epazote *(End of boil)*

In fermenter

Fill fermenter to 5 gallons (19 L) with
cool water

Fermentation

Yeast: WLP002 English AleYeast or Safale S-04
(68°F–72°F [20°C–22°C])

1 ounce (28 ml) vanilla extract, pure
(Day 4 of fermentation)

12 ounces (340 g) honey and 2 cups (475 ml)
hot water *(Day 4 of fermentation)*

Bottling

5 ounces (140 g) priming sugar

STARTING GRAVITY: 1.077

FINAL GRAVITY: 1.018

FINAL TARGET ABV: 8.5%

PROCESS

1. Fill your brewpot with 5½ gallons (21 L) of cool water.

2. Fill 2 grain bags with the crushed honey malt, the crushed rye malt, the crushed Special B, and the Black Patent malt.

2

3. Tie off the top, and place the bags in your brewpot.

3

4. Heat the pot and stir the water and grain bags every 5 minutes.

5. Just as the water reaches 170°F (77°F), pull out the grain bags using a large stirring spoon. Hold the bags above the brewpot for a minute allowing most of liquid to drain into the pot. Do not squeeze the grain bag.

6. As the water is beginning to boil, remove pot from heat.

7. Add your dry malt extract. Stir to prevent clumping and scorching on the bottom of the pot. Return pot to heat.

5a

7

5b

8. Allow the wort to come up to a boil. Reduce heat to a medium boil.

9. After preboiling for 5 minutes add your Perle hop pellets (bittering) and stir.

9

10. Start timing your 1-hour boil at the point that you make this hop addition.

11. Add the Irish moss and rock sugar 20 minutes before the end of the boil and stir for 1 minute.

11

12. Add the Hallertau hop pellets 15 minutes before the end of your 1-hour boil and stir for 1 minute.

13. At the 60-minute mark, turn off heat source and add the Mahlab and Epazote. Stir wort clockwise for 2 minutes as you build up a whirlpool effect. Stop stirring and allow wort to sit for 10 minutes.

13

14. Chill wort in cold water bath until it is under 75°F (24°C).

14

15. Transfer wort into fermenter or carboy.

16. Pitch yeast into the fermenter.

17. Add the Irish moss and rock sugar 20 minutes before the end of the boil and stir for 1 minute.

18. In 4 days, mix 2 cups (475 ml) hot water with the honey to dilute. Add honey mixture and vanilla to fermenter and stir well.

19. After 7 more days, check gravity to make sure it is not changing. Your beer should be ready to bottle.

21. Siphon the beer into a sterilized bottling bucket, add the water-diluted priming solution, and gently stir. Bottle and cap the beer.

22. Allow the beer to bottle condition for another 10 days and it should then be ready to drink.

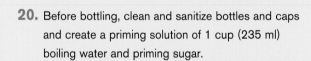

20. Before bottling, clean and sanitize bottles and caps and create a priming solution of 1 cup (235 ml) boiling water and priming sugar.

BASILISK

Jon Talkington, Dogfish Head Craft Brewery

Basilisk was the gold-medal winning metheglin at the 2011International Mazer Cup. A metheglin is a mead made with herbs or spices, in this case, sweet and lime basils. This semi-sweet mead is citrusy and clean with the lime accentuating the subtle basil flavor and aroma. As this is a mead, and honey is lacking in nutrients, the addition of yeast is vital, and the fermentation will be longer than that of a beer.

INGREDIENTS

Preboil tea at 150°F (66°C)

2 gallons (8 L) water

Grain bag

4 ounces (50 g) crushed 60 Lovibond crystal malt

8 ounces (100 g) crushed light chocolate malt

Beginning of Boil

2 quarts (320 g) chopped fresh sweet basil

2 quarts (320 g) chopped fresh lime basil

5 large limes, zested and juiced

In fermentation bucket

18 pounds (8.2 kg) of orange blossom honey

2 gallons (8 L) water

Fermentation

2 teaspoons(10 g) Lallemand 58 W3 wine yeast

1 teaspoon (5 g) yeast nutrient (Fermaid-K)

1 teaspoon (5 g) yeast nutrient (Fermaid-K)

STARTING GRAVITY: 1.078

FINAL GRAVITY: 1.016

FINAL TARGET ABV: 8%

IBUs: 25

PROCESS

1. Add 2 gallons (8 L) of water to your brewpot.

2. When the water begins to boil, remove the pot from the heat. Add the chopped sweet basil, lime basil, and lime juice and zest. Let steep for one hour.

3. Pour tea through a fine mesh sieve into a fermentation bucket.

4. Add honey and top up to the 5-gallon (19-L) mark with water. Allow to cool until temperature is 70°F (21°C).

5. Rehydrate the yeast in 4 oz (100 ml) of warm water (104°F [40°C]). Let stand 15 minutes without stirring, and then stir well to suspend the yeast.

6. Aerate the must for about 2 minutes, and then pitch the wine yeast. When fermentation has begun, add the first 5 grams of yeast nutrient. Mead needs to be fermented below 70°F (21°C).

7. When the specific gravity reaches 1.087 add the next 5 grams of yeast nutrient. Aerate for about a minute.

8. Allow the mead to ferment for 10–14 days, rack into a secondary fermenter–a clean glass carboy.

9. When clear, rack off of the sediment which usually takes 3–6 months. A fining agent may be added to speed up the clearing process. Bottle when clear and stable. Cork wine bottles for long-term aging.

CORNHOLIO

Short's Brewing Company

In 2011, Short's, Dogfish Head, and Three Floyds set out to brew an unusual concept beer that would highlight local ingredients from each participating brewery's region. The end result was Cornholio, a Baltic porter brewed with horehound, beach plums, and red popcorn. This odd combination of ingredients blends into a pleasing aroma of toasted popcorn with rich roasted malt and dark fruit. The initial flavors are of sweet plums that eventually become offset by the continued robust malt theme and the unique herbal accents from the horehound. A subtle burnt bitterness lingers in the aftertaste, but it's the surprisingly dry finish that ultimately leaves a lasting impression.

INGREDIENTS

Preboil tea at 150°F (66°C)

4 1/2 gallons (17 L) of cool water

16 ounces (455 g) crushed and toasted red popcorn kernels

16 ounces (455 g) crushed Ashburn Mild malt

16 ounces (455 g) crushed Bonlander Munich malt

16 ounces (455 g) crushed caramel 20L malt

4.8 ounces (136 g) crushed caramel 80L malt

3.2 ounces (90 g) crushed dark chocolate malt

0.5 ounce (14 g) crushed black malt

Grain bag

Boil

6 pounds (2.7 kg) light malt extract

0.64 ounces (20 g) Santiam hop pellets *(60 minutes)*

0.64 ounces (20 g) Santiam hop pellets *(30 minutes)*

0.32 ounces (10 g) Santiam hop pellets *(End of boil)*

0.32 ounces (10 g) Horehound *(End of boil)*

1¾ pounds (0.8 kg) pitted beach plums *(End of boil)*

Grain bag

Fermentation

Wyeast 2124 Bohemian Lager

Bottling

5 ounces (140 g) priming sugar

Extra equipment

Coffee grinder

Sheet pan

Blender

STARTING GRAVITY: 1.065

FINAL GRAVITY: 1.008

FINAL TARGET ABV: 7%

PROCESS

1. Add 2 gallons (8 L) of water to your brewpot.

2. Crush 16 ounces (455 g) red popcorn kernels using a coffee grinder. Spread the crushed red popcorn kernels out evenly onto a sheet pan. Toast the crushed kernels by baking them in the oven for 15 minutes at 350°F (180°C, gas mark 4).

3. Mix the toasted and crushed red popcorn kernels with the crushed specialty grains and place them into the grain bag. Tie off the top of the bag and place it into the brewpot containing 4.5 gallons (17 L) of cool water.

4. Heat the brewpot and stir the water and grain bag every 5 minutes.

5. Once the water reaches 170°F (77°C), remove the grain bag from the water and let the liquid from the bag drain into the brewpot. Do not squeeze the bag.

6. Once the water reaches a boil, remove the brewpot from heat.

7. Mix in the 6 pounds (2.7 kg) of light malt extract while stirring to prevent clumping and scorching on the bottom of the pot.

8. Heat the brewpot to boil. Once an even boil is achieved, add 0.64 oz (20 g) Santiam pellets. Start timing the 1 hour boil from this point.

9. With 30 minutes left in the boil, add 0.64 oz (20 g) Santiam pellets.

10. At the end of the 1-hour boil, remove the brewpot from heat. Add 0.32 oz (10 g) of Santiam pellets.

11. Place 0.32 oz (10 g) horehound into a grain bag, and steep in the brewpot at the end of boil for 10 minutes. After steeping for 10 minutes, remove the grain bag containing the horehound, allowing the liquid from it to drain into the brewpot. Do not squeeze the bag.

12. Puree 1¾ pounds (0.8 kg) of pitted beach plums in a blender. Add the beach plum puree into the brewpot after removing the horehound.

13. Stir the wort clockwise for 2 minutes to create a whirlpool action. Let the brewpot rest for 10 minutes.

14. Cool the wort in a cold water bath to 70°F (21°C).

15. Pour the wort into a plastic bucket fermenter.

16. Aerate the wort for 1 minute.

17. Pitch the yeast, aerate for another minute.

18. Fill the fermenter level to 5 gallons (19 L) with water.

19. Allow beer to ferment at 60°F (15°C) for 3 weeks, then rack beer off all fruit sediment into a secondary carboy.

20. Lager the beer for 3 weeks at below 50°F (10°C), then it will be ready to bottle.

21. Before bottling, sanitize a bottling bucket, bottles and caps.

22. Prepare a priming solution by mixing 5 ounces (140 g) of priming sugar with 1 cup (235 ml) of boiling water. Transfer beer from carboy to bottling bucket and mix in priming solution.

23. Bottle and cap.

24. Let beer age for at least 2 weeks before drinking.

FASTER, BIGGER, BETTER, BOLDER (GRADUALLY, QUIETLY, STEADILY)

Patrick Rue, Tyler King, and Sam Calagione (or The Bruery and Dogfish Head Teams)

The 2011 earthquake and tsunami in Japan inspired The Bruery and Dogfish Head to collaborate and brew a beer that incorporates American progressiveness with Japanese sensibility. We used several ingredients that were new to both breweries, such as kumquats and shichimi togarashi (Japanese five spice, a blend of all of the different spices listed in the ingredients). The beer expressed the personality of both breweries involved in its reserved extremism, and certainly has a bit of Japanese flair in its elegance and subtlety.

INGREDIENTS

Preboil

6 gallons (23 L) water

Beginning of boil

6.4 pounds (2.9 kg) pilsner liquid malt extract

2.13 pounds (1 kg) wheat liquid malt extract

1 pound (455 g) dried rice extract

0.25 ounces (7 g) Columbus hops

Boil (one hour)

1 pound (455 g) brown rice syrup *(0 minutes)*

10.5 ounces (300 g) kumquat puree *(0 minutes)*

Hop bag

2 ounces (60 g) ginger powder *(0 minutes)*

1.13 grams cayenne pepper *(0 minutes)*

1.13 grams white sesame seed *(0 minutes)*

1.13 grams black sesame seed (*(0 minutes)*

0.57 grams poppy seed *(0 minutes)*

0.3 grams nori *(0 minutes)*

Primary fermentation

Sake Yeast: Wyeast 4134 or White Labs 705

Secondary fermentation

Belgian Strong Ale: Wyeast 1388 or White Labs 570

Bottling

3–5 ounces (85–140) priming sugar

STARTING GRAVITY: 1.066

FINAL GRAVITY: 1.002

FINAL TARGET ABV: 8.25%

PROCESS

1. In a brew kettle, heat 6 gallons (27 L) of water to a boil. Remove kettle from heat and add all of the extract (but not the rice syrup!) and Columbus hops. Bring the wort to a boil for 1 hour.

2. During the boil place all of your spices in the hop bag and puree the kumquats.

3. At the end of the boil (60 minutes) remove the kettle from heat and add: kumquat puree, spices, and the brown rice syrup. Swirl the wort with a spoon to create a whirlpool, let rest for 10–15 minutes.

4. Cool the wort to 72°F (22°C) and rack to a fermenter leaving as much trub behind as possible.

5. Oxygenate the wort and pitch your primary yeast strain, let it ferment for 7 days.

6. Add your secondary yeast strain and let it ferment for another 7–10 days or as needed.

7. At bottling time, create a priming solution by combining 3–5 oz (85–140 g) of dextrose with 1 cup (235 ml) of boiling water.

8. Clean and sanitize a "bottling" bucket and add your priming solution.

9. Rack the finished beer into the bottling bucket and gently stir. Bottle and cap beer. Beer should be ready after two weeks at room temperature.

MIDAS TOUCHSTONE (ALL-GRAIN BREW)

Chris Wood and Eric Leypoldt, Dogfish Head Brewery

This brew blends a bit of the sweet (cherries and honey) and a bit of the sour (tart cherry juice and lacto/lambic yeast) to give a unique twist on an existing recipe. We used the base recipe of Midas Touch (see page 150), switched out one or two ingredients, added a few, and threw in a second yeast strain after primary fermentation. The end result will give you an American Wild Ale that is reminiscent of cherry pie.

INGREDIENTS

Preboil

4 gallons (15 L) mash water (158°F [70°C])

10 pounds (4.5 kg) ground 2-Row Pilsner Malt

2 pounds (900 g) ground wheat malt

1 tablespoon (15 g) gypsum

3–3 ½ gallons (11–13 L) sparge water (170°F [77°])

Boil

2 pounds (900 g) clover honey (@ 180°F [82°C])

¼ ounce (7 g) Simcoe hops *(60 minutes)*

1 pound (455 g) dark sweet cherries, pitted *(30 minutes)*

1 teaspoon (5 g) Irish moss *(15 minutes)*

2 quarts (2 L) tart cherry juice/concentrate *(end of boil)*

Primary fermentation

White Labs WLP001 or Wyeast 1056 ale yeast

Secondary fermentation

Wyeast 3278 lambic blend yeast

1 pound (455 g) pitted dark sweet cherries

1 ounce (28 g) Turkish cherry spice (Mahlab)

Bottling

5 ounces (140 g) priming sugar

STARTING GRAVITY: 1.090 (22 P)

FINAL GRAVITY: 1.020 (5 P)

FINAL TARGET ABV: 9–10%

IBU's: 12

PROCESS

1. Heat 4 gallons (15 L) of water to 158°F (70°C). Transfer to mash kettle (with false bottom screen), add gypsum, and stir in 2-Row Pilsner Malt and wheat malt.

2. Once all malt is mixed in, rest mash for 30 minutes, stirring occasionally. Target temperature is between 147°F–149°F (63°C–65°C).

3. Lautering process: Begin collecting wort in separate kettle until it becomes clear (approx. 15 minutes). Once wort becomes clear, stop collecting and add back into mash.

4. Runoff process: Once wort is clear, main wort collection can begin in kettle. Approximately 5 gallons (19 L) should be collected.

5. Sparge process: While collecting wort, the mash kettle will occasionally become dry. Have 3–3½ gallons (11–13 L) of sparge water at 170°F (77°C) on standby to add on top of grain bed during runoff. If runoff seems to slow, lightly stir the top third of the grain bed only. The object is to keep the grain bed lightly saturated (approx. 1 inch [2.5 cm] above grain bed) during runoff. The grain bed at the end of wort collection will most likely look dry.

6. Once all wort is collected, start to heat up wort to bring to a boil. (Boil time is 1 hour.)

7. The honey can be added at any time once kettle reaches 180°F (82°C).

8. When wort achieves boil add Simcoe hops.

9. At 30 minutes, put cherries in cheesecloth and add to boil.

10. With 15 minutes to go until end of boil, add Irish moss.

11. Stir in tart cherry juice at the very end of boil and before cooling wort.

12. Remove cherries and cool the wort. Transfer wort to fermentation vessel. Add ale yeast and ferment at room temperature. (70°F–74°F [21°–23°C]).

13. After vigorous fermentation subsides (approx 5–7 days), rack beer off yeast to a secondary fermentation vessel. Add the lambic yeast strain.

14. Once secondary yeast strain is added, put 1 pound (455 g) pitted dark sweet cherries in cheesecloth and put in fermentation vessel. Fermentation should continue for 5–7 more days. After fermentation is complete, allow beer to sit on yeast at room temperature for approximately 1 month. (The lengthy aging time on yeast allows for the beer to take on as much of the yeast characteristics as possible.)

15. About 1 day before cold conditioning beer (a refrigerator is fine to use), put 1 ounce (28 g) Mahlab into cheesecloth and put into fermentation vessel. Allow beer to condition for 12 to 14 days.

16. Before bottling, clean and sanitize bottles and caps and create a priming solution of 1 cup (235 ml) boiling water and priming sugar. Siphon beer into a sterilized bottling bucket, add the water-diluted priming solution, and gently stir. Bottle and cap beer. Beer will be ready to drink in about 2 weeks. *(Note: This beer may become more tart/sour as time goes on due to the lambic yeast strain)*

DEATH METAL

Tom Bastian, Homebrewer

Death Metal is a big-ole Imperial Stout with loads of Columbus, Amarillo, Centennial and Simcoe hops, a wide array of roasty toasty malts, honey, molasses, heaps of cold steeped coffee, and vanilla beans. The beer's in-your-face punch earned it the name Death Metal, and it lives up to the name with each of the flavorful ingredients head banging into your palate in succession. This beer was created by homebrewer Tom Bastian (http://bastianbrewing.blogspot.com) and was brewed as a brewpub exclusive at Dogfish Head Brewing and Eats along with Sam and Jason Weissberg as the Dogfish Head entry for the 2011 Great American Beer Festival pro-am competition in Denver. Tom won the Philly Beer Week's Extreme Homebrew Challenge in June of 2011 and his prize was to be able to brew with Dogfish Head at its pub in Rehoboth Beach Delaware. "There weren't any bad beers," Sam says. "But Tom's Death Metal stood out to me because you could taste or smell each of the special ingredients that he mentioned in the description, but none of them was overwhelming. Extreme for me is extremely flavorful, extremely memorable, not just extremely strong. And he had all of that."

INGREDIENTS

Preboil tea

Preboil tea at 150°F (65°C)

7 gallons (26 L) of water

Grain bags (you may need a couple)

1½ pounds (680 g) of roasted barley

½ pound (225) Black Patent malt

1 pound (455 g) chocolate malt

1 pound (455 g) Crystal 120

1 pound (455 g) flaked oats

Boil

9 pound (4 kg) of extra-light dried malt extract *(90 minutes)*

1 pound (455 g) of wheat dried malt extract *(90 minutes)*

1 pound (455 g) of orange blossom honey *(5 minutes)*

1/2 pound (225) black strap molasses *(1 minute)*

1.5 ounces (43 g) of Columbus hops *(60 minutes)*

1 ounce (28 g) of Centennial hops *(15 minutes)*

2 ounces (57 g) of Simcoe hops *(5 minutes)*

2 ounces (57 g) of Amarillo hops *(Flame out)*

Fermentation

Wyeast 1056 or WLP001 – American Ale Yeast

STARTING GRAVITY: 1.098

FINAL GRAVITY: 1.025

FINAL TARGET ABV: 9.9%

IBU's: 100

Deluxe Brews

PROCESS

1. In a brew kettle, heat 7 gallons (26.5 L) of water to 150°F (65°C). In a grain bag (or a few), add the crushed roasted barley, black patent, chocolate, Crystal 120, and flaked oats. Allow to steep for 15 minutes.

2. Remove the grain bag and bring water to a boil.

3. Remove from heat and add the light malt extract and wheat extract.

4. Return to a boil.

5. Add 1.5 oz (43 g) of Columbus hops and boil for 60 minutes.

6. Add 1 oz (28 g) of Centennial hops and boil for 15 minutes.

7. Add the Orange Blossom Honey and 2 oz (57 g) of Simcoe hops and boil for 5 minutes.

8. Remove from heat and add 2 oz (57 g) of Amarillo hops.

9. Cool to 70°F (21°C), oxygenate, and rack to the fermenter.

10. Pitch yeast and ferment at 68°F (20°C).

11. When fermentation is complete, rack to secondary vessel for 2 weeks.

12. Add 1 vanilla bean to fermentor (split bean and soak in vodka over night before adding to the carboy). Pour in both the bean and vodka. Let sit in secondary for two weeks.

13. Take ¾ pound of Ethiopian Yirgacheffe coffee and do a course grind on the beans. Take a sanitized pot and add 2 quarts (2 L) of cold water. Using a sanitized spoon mixed in coffee grinds. Cover pot and let sit in fridge for 24 hours. Use a sanitized French press to remove the grinds and poured the cold pressed coffee into a bottling bucket. (Tom and Dogfish Head used coffee from College Coffee Roasters, Lancaster, Pennsylvania.) Beans can be ordered online at www.collegecoffeeroasters.com). Transfer your beer out of primary onto the cold-pressed coffee and bottle. Be careful to pour slowly so not to introduce additional oxygen into the bottling bucket

REDBEARD'S CPA

Shawn Hager, Xtreme Brewing

If you like your hop flavor and aroma intense and light at the same time, this Citra pale ale is definitely for you. There's an epic amount of Citra hops in the boil with a final shot of dry Citra hops in the secondary to create an outstanding American pale ale. This is a hop-head's dream, with 6 ounces (170 g) of Citra in a 5-gallon (19-L) batch."

INGREDIENTS

Preboil tea

5 gallons (19 L) cool water

8 ounces (230 g) 10 L Crystal malt, crushed

8 ounces (230 g) 20 L Crystal malt, crushed

8 ounces (230 g) Victory malt, crushed

8 ounces (230 g) CaraMunich malt, crushed

2 grain bags

Boil

7 pounds (3.2 kg) light dry malt extract *(65 minutes)*

2 ounces (57 g) Magnum hops *(60 minutes)*

½ ounce (14 g) Citra hops *(20 minutes)*

½ ounce (14 g) Citra hops *(15 minutes)*

1 teaspoon (5 g) Irish moss *(15 minutes)*

½ ounce (14 g) Citra hops *(10 minutes)*

½ ounce (14 g) Citra hops *(5 minutes)*

1 ounce (28 g) Citra hops *(End of boil)*

In fermenter

Fill the fermenter to the 5-gallon (19-L) mark with cool water, if needed

Fermentation

Yeast: Safale S-04 or Wyeast 1187 Ringwood Ale yeast

Secondary

3 ounces (85 g) Citra Hops (dry hopping)

Bottling

2 cups (470 g) water

5 ounces (140 g) priming sugar

Note: Time notations beside items indicate the length of time they are in the boil or when they are used during the boil or the day that item is added or used. If you are not able to boil the full volume of this beer, use only as much water as you can safely boil in your pot.

STARTING GRAVITY: 1.075

FINAL GRAVITY: 1.021

FINAL TARGET ABV: 7.5%

PROCESS

1. In a brew kettle, start to heat 5 gallons (19 L) of cool water.

2. In the grain bags, add the four crushed grains to the cool/cold water.

3. Allow to steep until the water reaches 170°F (77°C). Occasionally move the bag to improve water circulation to facilitate sugar and flavor extraction.

4. Remove the grain bags and bring water to a boil.

5. Remove pot from heat and add the malt extract. Stir well to dissolve malt extract.

6. Return to heat and bring to a boil.

7. After 5 minutes, add 2 ounces (57 g) of magnum hops. Start the 60 minute time.

8. At the 20 minute mark, add ½ ounce (14 g) Citra.

9. At the 15 minute mark, add ½ ounce (14 g) Citra and Irish moss

10. At the 10 minute mark, add ½ ounce (14 g) Citra.

11. At the 5 minute mark, add ½ ounce (14 g) Citra.

12. After 60 minutes, remove the kettle from the heat.

PROCESS

13. After adding 1 ounce (28 g) of Citra hops, stir the wort to create a whirlpool. Cover and allow the hops to steep and settle for 15 to 20 minutes.

14. Cool the wort to 70°F (21°C) and pour into a fermenter leaving most of the solids behind in the kettle. (It's okay to get some of the sediment into the fermenter as it is beneficial to yeast health.) Aerate as you pour or rock fermenter as needed. Add water if needed to bring up to the 5-gallon (19-L) mark.

15. Pitch the cooled wort with ale yeast and ferment at around 66°F–70°F (19°C–21°C).

16. After 5 to 7 days, rack the beer to the secondary fermenter (5-gallon [19-L] carboy) leaving behind as much yeast and trub as possible. Add 3 ounces (85 g) of Citra hops. Top up to 5 gallons (19 L) with water if needed.

17. Allow beer to condition in secondary for 1 to 2 weeks. Rock carboy occasionally to stir up hops that have accumulated around the top of the beer.

18. Before bottling boil priming sugar in one cup of water. Add to racked beer. Gently stir to disperse sugar. Sanitize bottles and caps. Fill bottles to 1″–1½″ (2.5–4 cm) from top and cap.

19. Allow the beer to bottle condition for two weeks and it should then be fully carbonated.

SMOKIN' CHERRY BOMB (OR CHERRY BOMB)

Doug Griffith, Carl Herbst, Josh Campbell, and Jerry Franklin, Xtreme Brewing

This is a triple cherry bomb threat, forging the cherry power of sour cherries, Turkish cherry pits, and cherry extract for a mini-explosion of sweet cherries that slides right under the layer of luscious smokiness from the smoked cherry wood malt, leaving you with a complex smoky-sweet flavor that lingers … just long enough. The smoked malt is optional and may be omitted if the smokiness is not desired.

INGREDIENTS

Preboil tea

4½ gallons (17 L) cool water

8 ounces (230 g) wheat malt, crushed

8 ounces (230 g) Munich malt, crushed

1 pound (455 g) Briess smoked malt, crushed (optional)

2 grain bags

2 teaspoons (8 g) gypsum

Boil

6.6 pounds (3 kg) light malt extract *(65 minutes)*

1 ounce (28 g) Northern Brewer hop pellets (bittering) *(60 minutes)*

½ ounce (14 g) Fuggles or Willamette hop pellets (flavor) *(20 minutes)*

½ ounce (14 g) Tettnanger hop pellets (aroma) *(10 minutes)*

1 teaspoon Irish moss *(10 minutes)*

½ ounce (14 g) Mahalab (dried Turkish cherry pits) *(End of boil)*

6 pounds (2.7 kg) sour cherries, crushed or

5 pounds (2.3 kg) frozen sour cherries or

1 pound (455 g) dried sour cherries *(During cooling)*

4 teaspoon Pectic enzyme *(During cooling)*

In fermenter

Fill fermenter to 5 gallons (19 L) with cool water.

Fermentation

Yeast: Fermentis Safale S-04 or White Labs WLP002 English ale

Bottling

1 bottle (4 ounces or 118 ml) cherry extract

5 ounces (140 g) priming sugar

STARTING GRAVITY: 1.066

FINAL GRAVITY: 1.016

FINAL TARGET ABV: 6.5%

PROCESS

1. Fill your brewpot with 4½ gallons (17 L) of cool water.

2. Fill a grain bag with the crushed grains. Tie off the top and place the bag in your brewpot.

3. Add 2 teaspoons (8 g) gypsum to the water.

4. Heat the pot, stirring the water and grain bag every 5 minutes.

5. As the water reaches 170°F (77°C), pull out the specialty grain bag using a large stirring spoon. Hold the bag(s) above the brewpot allowing most of the liquid to drain into the pot. Do not squeeze the grain bag.

6. As the water is beginning to boil, remove from the heat.

7. Add your malt extract syrup. Stir well to prevent clumping and scorching of the malt extract.

8. Return the pot to the heat. Allow the wort to come up to a boil.

9. After preboiling for 5 minutes, add your Northern Brewer hop pellets and stir.

10. Start timing your 1-hour boil at the point that you make this hop addition.

11. Add the flavor hops (Fuggle or Willamette) 20 minutes before the end of your boil and stir for 1 minute.

12. Add the Tettnanger hop pellets and the Irish moss 10 minutes before the end of the boil and stir for 1 minute.

13. At the 1-hour mark of your boil, turn off heat source and add the Mahalab. Let the beer come down below 170°F (77°C). Placing the brewpot in a water bath will speed up the cooling time. Add your cherries. You don't want to add the fruit to boiling beer as the high temperature will set the natural fruit pectin which may adversely affect the clarity of your beer. Stir wort clockwise for 2 minutes as you build up a whirlpool effect. Stop stirring, cover, and allow wort to sit for 10 minutes.

14. Chill wort in cold water bath until it is under 75°F (24°C).

15. For the primary fermentation, a plastic bucket fermenter would be easier to use for this brew. It will be difficult to get the cherries in and out of the glass carboy. Pour the cooled wort and cherries into the fermenter, if possible, leave behind some of the sediment. To aerate, pour your wort back and forth between the plastic fermenter and your sanitized bottling bucket 4 or 5 times.

16. Add the pectic enzyme.

17. Top up to the 5-gallon (19-L) mark with cool water. Pitch yeast into fermenter. If using liquid yeast, aerate for another minute.

18. After primary fermentation is over (your airlock has stopped bubbling), if using the plastic fermenter, transfer your beer into the sanitized carboy leaving behind all of the fruit, pits, and yeast solids that have settled to the bottom; if using a carboy, transfer your beer to the sanitized bottling bucket, clean the carboy and move the beer back to the carboy.

19. In about two weeks your beer should be ready to package. Rack your beer to another container to leave all sediment behind. Boil priming sugar in one cup of water. Add to racked beer. Add the bottle of cherry flavor. Stir to disperse sugar and flavoring. Sanitize bottles and caps. Fill bottles to 1″–1½″ (2.5–4 cm) from top and cap.

20. Allow the beer to bottle condition for another two weeks and it should then be fully carbonated.

FRUIT GRUIT

Tod Mott, Tyler Jones, and Sam Calagione, Portsmouth (NH) Brewery

Needless to say, this medieval beer style has been around for a long time and has no real guidelines as far as style, flavor, ingredients, and color—so the sky is the limit and the only parameters are the ones in your imagination. Collaborating with Sam was the perfect fit for us at the Portsmouth Brewery, in Portsmouth, New Hampshire, because we've brewed just about everything under the sun and needed a style we weren't familiar with. With the help of Paul Sayler from Burlington Hearth & Flatbread and Zero Gravity Brewing Co., in Burlington, Vermont; Tom Baker from Earth Bread & Brewery, in Philadelphia, and Will Meyers, from Cambridge Brewing Co. in Cambridge, Massachusetts, we were able to devise a recipe to which the three of us could then tweak. Tyler and I met with Sam and devised this recipe. The base beer was a brown porter in which we incorporated the herbs and fruit.

INGREDIENTS

Mash

57% 2 row "plains" malted barley (like Metcalf)

25% English 2 row malted barley

5% flaked barley

4.5% malted wheat

3% 77° English Crystal malt

2% 120° caramel malt

1% Weyermann Carafa #2 D/H

1% Chocolate malt

1% Aromatic malt

0.5% Black Patent malt

PROCESS

Mash: The use of single temperature infusion mashing was the method to get the fermentable sugars from the basic porter recipe. We doughed in at 164°F (73°C) and stabilized at 153°F (67°C) where we let the enzymes break down the starches to sugars for 45 minutes. Upon completion of saccrification, we recirculated (Vorlauff) the extract for 10 minutes to clarify the wort. Once clarified, we started our run off and collected the wort. We were looking for 14 degrees Plato.

Boil: The extract was boiled for one hour. Because the great state of New Hampshire dictates that all beer must have hops in any given beer recipe we complied with the state regulations. Though the hop charge was negligible we did add about the equivalent of 14 IBUs. So, our boiling hops of choice were German Magnum for the duration of the boil. During the boil we added the herbs as well as 30 pounds of Milton DE finest plums from Fifer Orchards with 10 minutes left in the boil. The plums were pitted, smashed and placed in a stainless steel cage, usually used for whole leaf hops, and the cage was placed into the kettle for the final 10 minutes of the boil. The herbs used were: ½ pound (225 g) Yarrow and ½ pound (225 g) Sweet Gale and about 4 ounces (115 g) of Mugwort all of which came from Burlington, Vermont. These herbs were placed into a muslin sack and put into the boil with 10 minutes left in the boil, at the same time the plums went into the kettle. The herbs added at the whirlpool addition were: ½ pound (225 g) yarrow, ½ pound (225 g) sweet gale, 6 ounces mugwort (again from Burlington VT.) as well as some herbs procured by John Forte, from Strawbery Banke here in Portsmouth, New Hampshire, who brought 10 ounces (280 g) local wormwood, 10 ounces (280 g) fresh horhound and 4 ounces (115 g) fresh rosemary. We also added 10 ounces (280 g) of lavender (from Lavender Fields at Harrington Manor LLC. Milton, Delaware). Tom Baker indicated to me that the herb sack is what is called the gruit and should travel from the kettle to the fermenter in order to incorporate the herb into the fermentation process. With that in mind we moved the herb sack from the kettle after knock out and into the fermenter where the yeast was added and fermentation started shortly after pitching.

Fermentation: Fermentation was achieved with a California-style ale yeast fermented at 68°F (20°C). The primary fermentation took about 4 days and we let the fermentation continue another 3 days where we added the second dose of fruit: peaches from Milton DE's Fifer Orchards. We blanched the peaches, halved the peaches, pitted the peaches then pureed the peaches. We brought the puree to 150°F (65°C) to Pasteurize the fruit and let the puree cool overnight. The puree was then added to the fermentation tank where a secondary fermentation occurred. After another 6 days of fermentation the tank was turned to 45°F (7°C). for slow cooling. Three days later the tank was turned to 38°F (3°C) for conditioning. The conditioning period was about another 8 days. Yeast was racked after the maturing beer reached 38°F (3°C). and some natural carbonation occurred. The beer was racked into a serving vessel where the fruit gruit aged another week. The CO_2 levels did not reach the intended levels and some "polishing" needed to be done to improve the CO_2 levels. The beer was quite unique and had some seriously good qualities about it.

WET HOP AMERICAN SUMMER

Ryan Harvey, Tim Hawn, and Sam Calagione, Dogfish Head Craft Brewery

This is a homebrew version of our annual cult classic, Wet Hop American Summer. This is an English ale using fresh cascade hops. The beer is brewed twenty-four hours after the hops were picked from the vine. If you grow your own hops or if you can source fresh hops from a homebrew shop or a friend, this is a must try beer to brew. Fresh hops add a unique flavor that you cannot get from hops that have been processed. A note about using fresh hops: It may seem like you are using a lot of hops, however these are unkilned hops that contain a lot of moisture. Typically, a ratio of around 6:1 wet vs. processed hops is used to obtain the same bitterness

INGREDIENTS

Preboil tea

6 gallons (23 L) of water at 150°F (65°C)

Grain bag

12 ounces (340 g) Briess Carapils malt

8 ounces (230 g) caramel/crystal malt 120°L

Boil

8 pounds (3.6 kg) light/pale malt extract syrup

2 mesh bags

7½ ounces (215 g) fresh wet cascade hops *(60 minutes)*

5 ounces (140 g) fresh wet cascade hops *(15 minutes)*

14 ounces (400 g) fresh wet cascade hops (in hop back or lauter vessel)

Whirlfloc or Irish moss *(10 minutes)*

Fermentation

Yeast: British pale ale

Bottling

5 ounces (140 g) priming sugar

STARTING GRAVITY: 1.064

FINISHING GRAVITY: 1.012

FINAL TARGET ABV: 7%

PROCESS

1. In a brew kettle, heat up 6 gallons (23 L) of water to 150°F (65°C). In a grain bag, add 12 oz (340 g) of Briess Carapils malt and 8 oz (230 g) of caramel/Crystal 120°L malt. Steep for 15 minutes then remove bag.

2. Bring brew kettle to a boil, while waiting; begin stuffing grain bags with your fresh hop cones. If you have something heavy and sanitary (we used a bunch of stainless steel parts) add it to the bag to help keep it from floating. If you don't have anything, be sure to keep poking the bag into the wort during the boil using a spoon or paddle.

3. Once boiling, remove from heat and add 8 pounds (3.6 kg)of light/pale malt extract. Return to boil.

4. Once a good boil has been achieved, add your first hop addition of 7½ oz (215 g) cascade hops in a mesh bag.

5. After 45 minutes add your second bag (5 oz [140 g]) of hop cones.

6. After 50 minutes, add your whirlfloc or Irish moss.

7. At the end of 60 minutes, transfer your wort to another vessel containing your last addition (14 oz [400 g]) of hops. If you have a way of straining from this last vessel, leave the hops loose rather than in a bag, to get more wort-to-hop surface contact.

8. Let sit on hops for 10 minutes.

9. After 10 minutes transfer work to fermentation vessel.

10. Once the wort is cooled to 74°F (23°C), pitch your yeast and stir or rock the carboy to ensure proper wort/yeast aeration.

11. Once primary fermentation is done (6–8 days) transfer to secondary fermentation vessel.

12. Allow to age another 10 to 14 days.

13. Prior to bottling, have clean and sanitized bottles and caps ready. Add priming sugar to 1 cup (235 ml) of boiling water. Siphon beer into bottling bucket, stir in priming solution, and begin bottling.

14. Wait 2 to 3 weeks and then enjoy.

COFFEE & CREAM STOUT

Jerry Franklin

A dark, luscious American-style creamy milk stout with plenty of coffee flavor and a hint of sweetness from the lactose (milk sugar). The dark-roasted coffee is cold steeped to avoid the bitterness of the popular hot-brewed versions. This combination of lactose and cold-steeped coffee provides a smoother full-bodied taste great for a cold winter day.

INGREDIENTS

Preboil

4½ gallons (17 L) cool water

4 ounces (115 g) black patent malt, crushed

4 ounces (115 g) roasted barley, crushed

4 ounces (115 g) Debittered Black

Grain bag

Boil

7 pounds (3.2 kg) dark dry malt extract *(65 minutes)*

½ ounce (14 g) Magnum pellet hops (bittering) *(60 minutes)*

¼ ounce (7 g) Magnum pellet hops (flavor) *(30 minutes)*

¾ ounces (21 g) Centennial pellet hops (flavor/aroma) *(10 minutes)*

1 teaspoon (5 g) Irish moss *(15 minutes)*

1 pound (455 g) lactose *(End of boil)*

In fermenter

Fill fermenter to 5 gallons (19 L) with cool water

Fermentation

1 Fermentis Safale S-04 or White Labs WLP028 English Ale Yeast at 68°F–72°F (20°C–22°C)

1 cup (235 ml) dark roasted coffee 5th day of fermentation

Enough water to cover crushed coffee, approx. 1 quart (1 L) 5th day of fermentation

Grain bag (for straining coffee) 5th day of fermentation

Bottling

5 ounces (140 g) priming sugar

STARTING GRAVITY: 1.072

FINISHING GRAVITY: 1.016

FINAL TARGET ABV: 7%

PROCESS

1. Fill your brewpot with 4½ gallons (17 L) of cool water.

2. Fill grain bag with the crushed black patent malt, the crushed roasted barley, and the crushed Debittered Black.

3. Tie off the top and place the bag in your brewpot.

4. Heat the pot and stir the water and grain bags every 5 minutes.

5. Just as the water reaches 170°F (77°C), pull out the grain bags using a large stirring spoon. Hold the bags above the brewpot for a minute allowing most of liquid to drain into the pot. Do not squeeze the grain bag.

6. As the water is beginning to boil, remove pot from heat.

7. Add all your malt extract. Stir to prevent clumping and scorching on the bottom of the pot. Return pot to heat.

8. Allow the wort to come up to a boil.

9. After preboiling for 5 minutes add your bittering hop pellets and stir.

10. Start timing your 1-hour boil at the point that you make this hop addition.

11. Add the flavor hop pellets 30 minutes before the end of your 1-hour boil and stir for 1 minute.

12. Add Irish moss 15 minutes before the end of the boil and stir for 1 minute.

13. Add the Centennial hop pellets 10 minutes before end of boil and stir for 1 minute.

14. At the 60-minute mark, turn off heat source and add the lactose. Stir wort clockwise for 2 minutes as you build up a whirlpool effect. Stop stirring and allow wort to sit for 10 minutes.

15. Chill wort in cold water bath until it is under 75°F (24°C).

16. Transfer wort into fermenter or carboy.

17. Top up the fermenter to the 5-gallon (19-L) mark with cool water.

18. Pitch yeast into fermenter. If using liquid yeast, aerate (rock the baby or stir) for 1 minute.

19. In about 5 days, crush coffee, put in jar, cover with cold water. Steep cold for 12 to 24 hours. Strain with bag. Add liquid to fermenter.

20. In about 5 days, your beer should be ready to package.

21. Before bottling, clean and sanitize bottles and caps and create a priming solution of 1 cup (235 ml) boiling water and priming sugar.

22. Siphon the beer into a sterilized bottling bucket, add the water-diluted priming solution, and gently stir. Bottle and cap the beer.

23. Allow the beer to bottle condition for another 10 days and it should then be ready to drink.

DIRTY BANANA

Doug Griffith, Xtreme Brewing

This is a complex medium-amber brew that transforms the unusual mix of ingredients into a smooth surprise. The great mouth feel goes just right with the feel of the higher alcohol. The banana flavor from the T-58 yeast pulls in the hint of chocolate and red pepper. Trade some of the banana tones for light citrus ones with a switch to the S-33 yeast.

INGREDIENTS

Preboil tea

5 gallons (19 L) cool water

Boil

4 pounds (1.8 kg) golden light dry malt extract *(65 minutes)*

4 pounds (1.8 kg) amber dry malt extract *(65 minutes)*

1 ounce (28 g) Cluster hop pellets (bittering) *(60 minutes)*

½ ounce (14 g) Perle hop pellets (flavor) *(30 minutes)*

1 teaspoon (5 g) Irish moss *(20 minutes)*

½ ounce (14 g) Willamette hop pellets (aroma) *(End of boil)*

¾ pound (340 g) honey *(End of boil)*

1 pound (455 g) corn sugar *(End of boil)*

.05 ounce crushed red pepper *End of boil*)

3 ounces (85 g) cocoa powder *(End of boil)*

In fermenter

Fill fermenter with 5 gallons (19 L) cool water

Fermentation

Yeast: Safale T-58, S-33 or White Labs WLP565 Saison

Bottling

2 cups (475 ml) water

5 ounces (140 g) priming sugar

STARTING GRAVITY: 1.088

FINISHING GRAVITY: 1.016

FINAL TARGET ABV: 9.5%

PROCESS

1. Fill your brewpot with 5 gallons (19 L) of cool water.

2. Heat the pot.

3. As the water is beginning to boil, remove pot from heat.

4. Add your dry malt extract stirring well to remove most of the clumps. Return to heat.

5. Allow the wort to come to a boil.

6. After preboiling for 5 minutes add your Cluster hop pellets (bittering) and stir.

7. Start timing your 1-hour boil at the point that you make this hop addition.

8. Add the Perle hops 30 minutes from the end of boil.

9. Add the Irish moss 20 minutes from the end of the boil and stir for 1 minute.

10. Turn off heat source at 60 minutes of your boil and add the Willamette aroma hops, and stir for 1 minute.

11. Add the corn sugar, honey, crushed red pepper, and cocoa, and stir wort clockwise for 2 minutes as you build up a whirlpool effect.

12. Stop stirring and allow wort to sit for 10 minutes.

13. Chill wort in cold water bath until it is under 75°F (24°C).

14. Transfer wort into fermenter.

15. Top up wort to 5-gallon (19-L) level with cold water

16. Pitch yeast into fermenter. Stir for a minute if using the liquid yeast.

17. Let ferment until done, 10 to 14 days.

18. Rack, add priming sugar, bottle and cap.

19. Allow the beer to bottle condition for about 2 weeks and it should then be ready to drink.

FRUITCAKE

Doug Griffith, Carl Herbst, Jerry Franklin, and Joe Gordon, Xtreme Brewing

Finally, there's a fruitcake that you'll hoard for yourself. We dumped a copious amount of fruit in the brew pot—dried pineapple, cherries, cranberries, and raisins plus crystallized ginger and calmed it all into velvety smoothness with chamomile. A rich, full-bodied ale that gets even better with age ... just like its namesake.

INGREDIENTS

Preboil tea

4 ½ gallons (17 L) cool water

1 pound (455 g) Carapils malt, crushed

Grain bag

2 teaspoons (8 g) gypsum

Boil

6 pounds (2.7 g) light dry malt extract *(65 minutes)*

1 ounce (28 g) Kent Golding hop pellets (bittering) *(60 minutes)*

1 teaspoon (5 g) Irish moss *(10 minutes before the end of boil)*

2 grain bags to hold fruit

4 ounces (115 g) dried cranberries *(End of boil)*

4 ounces (115 g) dried pineapples *(End of boil)*

4 ounces (115 g) dried cherries *(End of boil)*

4 ounces (115 g) dried raisins *(End of boil)*

4 ounces (115 g) crystallized ginger, cut into pea size pieces *(End of boil)*

1 1/2 ounces (45 g) chamomile *(End of boil)*

In fermenter

Fill fermenter to 5 gallons (19 L) with cool water

Fermentation

Yeast: American Ale Yeast , Safale US-05 or White Labs WLP 001

1 teaspoon Irish moss *(10 minutes)*

Bottling

5 ounces (140 g) priming sugar

STARTING GRAVITY: 1.056

FINISHING GRAVITY: 1.015

FINAL TARGET ABV: 7%

PROCESS

1. Fill your brewpot with 4½ gallons (17 L) of cool water.

2. Fill a grain bag with the crushed Carapils malt. Tie off the top and place the bag in your brewpot.

3. Add two teaspoons gypsum to the water.

4. Heat the pot and stir the water and grain bag every 5 minutes.

5. As the water begins to reach 170°F (77°C), pull out the grain bag using a large stirring spoon. Hold the bag above the brewpot for a minute allowing most of the liquid to drain into the pot. Do not squeeze the grain bag.

6. As the water is beginning to boil, remove pot from the heat.

7. Add all your malt extract. Stir to prevent clumping and scorching on the bottom of the pot. Return to the heat.

8. Allow the wort to come up to a boil.

9. After preboiling for 5 minutes add your bittering hop pellets and stir.

10. Start timing your 1-hour boil at the point that you make this hop addition.

11. Add the Irish moss 10 minutes before the end of the boil and stir for 1 minute.

12. At the 60-minute mark of your boil place all the dried fruits, ginger, and chamomile in the two grain bags, add to pot, and turn off heat source. If using a carboy for fermentation, the fruit may be pureed and added to the boil pot.

13. Stir wort clockwise for 2 minutes as you build up a whirlpool effect.

14. Stop stirring and allow wort to sit for 10 minutes.

15. Chill wort in cold water bath until it is under 75°F (24°C).

16. Transfer wort (if using pureed fruit include all sediment in pot) and fruit filled grain bags into fermenter, aerate (rock the baby) for 1 minute.

17. Top up to the 5-gallon (19-L) mark with cool water.

18. Pitch yeast into fermenter. If using liquid yeast aerate for another minute.

19. In about ten days your beer should be ready to package. Rack your beer to another container to leave all sediment behind. Boil priming sugar in one cup of water. Add to racked beer. Stir to disperse sugar. Sanitize bottles and caps. Fill bottles to 1″–1½″ (2.5–4 cm) from top and cap.

20. Allow the beer to bottle condition for another ten days and it should then be ready to drink or keep longer for a special occasion.

PSRT (PARSLEY, SAGE, ROSEMARY & THYME)

Doug Griffith, Xtreme Brewing

This is a light, refreshing Belgian saison. The balance of this classic combination of herbs lets parsley, rosemary, and thyme each come through in the taste finishing with the softness of sage. This beer may be fermented warmer than normal due to the herbs. Additional pepper and floral notes created by the yeast at warmer fermentation temperature add another dimension to the taste. If you keg, we find this beer to be exceptionally light and refreshing when force carbonated and served as fresh as possible, 5 days or so after brewing. Wet versus processed hops is used to obtain the same bitterness

INGREDIENTS

Preboil tea

5 gallons (17 L) cool water

Boil

6 pounds (2.7 kg) Pilsen light dry malt extract *(65 minutes)*

1 ounce (28 g) Willamette pellet hops (bittering) *(60 minutes)*

1 teaspoon parsley flakes, dry *(End of boil)*

½ teaspoon sage, rubbed *(End of boil)*

½ teaspoon rosemary leaves, dry *(End of boil)*

1 teaspoon thyme leaves, dry *(End of boil)*

In fermenter

Fill with cool water to 5-gallon (19-L) mark.

Fermentation

Fermentis S-33 or T-58 dry yeast or White Labs WLP565 Saison liquid yeast

Bottling

5 ounces (140 g) priming sugar

STARTING GRAVITY: 1.062

FINISHING GRAVITY: 1.010

FINAL TARGET ABV: 6%

PROCESS

1. Fill a brewpot with 5 gallons (19 L) of cool water. If your pot is not large enough, use at least ½ gallons (5.7 L) or more if possible.

2. Heat the pot.

3. As the water is beginning to boil, remove from heat.

4. Add the dry malt extract. Stir to prevent clumping and scorching on the bottom of the pot.

5. Return the brewpot to the heat. Allow the wort to come up to a boil.

6. After pre-boiling for 5 minutes add your Willamette hop pellets for bittering and stir.

7. Start timing your 1 hour boil at the point that you make this hop addition.

8. At the 60 minute mark of your boil add your herbs and turn off heat source.

9. Stir wort clockwise for 2 minutes as you build up a whirlpool effect. Stop stirring and allow wort to sit for 10 minutes.

10. Chill wort in cold water bath until it is between 75°F and 85°F (24°C and 29°C). Because of the herbs used in this beer, spicy and floral notes are expected. This beer can be fermented warmer than most beers, which adds to the herb, pepper, and floral notes. Fermentation temps may be as high as 85°F (29°C). At this temp, the beer will be ready to bottle or keg in 5 days.

11. Transfer wort into the fermenter, aerate (rock the baby) for 1 minute.

12. Top up the fermenter with cool water to the 5 gallon (19-L) mark.

13. Pitch yeast into fermenter. If using liquid yeast stir well.

14. In about 10 days your beer should be ready to package. Rack your beer to another container to leave all sediment behind.

15. Boil priming sugar in one cup of water. Add to racked beer. Stir to disperse sugar.

16. Sanitize bottles and caps. Fill bottles to 1″–1½″ (2.5–4 cm) from top and cap.

17. Allow the beer to bottle condition for another two weeks and it should then be fully carbonated.

CHAPTER 11

Beer Pairings and Dinners

NOW THAT YOU HAVE a good understanding of how to make beer, it's time to discuss the finer points of why you chose to brew in the first place: enjoyment. Making and drinking good beer is a social activity. Whether it's being served at a full-blown, four-course meal or at a simple tasting event, beer is every bit as complex, diverse, and complementary to food as wine. It is as deserving of a place on the finest linen-clad tables as it is on picnic tables. In fact, certain foods, particularly cheese and chocolate, work much better with beer than wine. I always enjoy hanging out with people who bring their joy for life into their work—who are so passionate about what they do that it is better defined as a calling than a job. Robert Aguilera of Formaggio Kitchen in Boston and Garrett Oliver, the brewmaster of Brooklyn Brewery in New York, are two people who have incorporated a love of beer and food into all aspects of their lives. In this chapter, they provide guidelines on how to host cheese and beer and chocolate and beer tastings at home. These events can be as simple or as complex as you wish to make them. Again, the bottom line is that you are creating an environment in which to interact with and enjoy great friends, great food, and great beer.

Beer and Cheese Pairing

Robert Aguilera, Formaggio Kitchen

I have the luxury of working with well over 400 different cheeses throughout the year. Though selecting cheeses to pair with beer is not a big chore for me anymore, I often see the deer-in-the-headlights look from customers who don't know where to begin. I was the same way five years ago.

If you are trying to train your palate and refine your understanding of food pairings, do not attempt to do so without a few friends. The simple reason for this advice is that every person tastes food differently. Therefore, in order to truly hone your food pairing thinking, it helps to debate the flavors and the combinations with your close friends. Hey, after a few pints, they'll tell you what they really think. That being said, if you want to host a beer and cheese pairing that everyone will truly learn something from, dole out the beer in 1 or 2 ounce (28 or 60 ml) pours and have a heap of bread nearby to munch on. You want the discussion to be lively, not sloppy.

Beer and cheese tastings done at home are exciting. The two share common threads in their beginnings: grain and a fermentation process. Beer and cheese are also spiritually linked by those Trappist monks of the Middle Ages who devoted their time and focus to developing both food products. Beer and cheese are the great levelers; no matter where you came from, what kind of upbringing you had, beer and cheese will make you smile, even more so if they pair perfectly. So, how do you have a beer and cheese pairing at home? It can seem daunting at first, but I have found two ways of presenting my pairing parties that have helped me quickly learn the most.

First, there is the less is more approach to pairing. In other words, if you have never hosted a beer and cheese pairing and you really want to wow your friends and start a new tradition, the best way to begin is to pick your favorite beer and four cheeses. This pairing helps you understand all of the possible flavors in your favorite beer by introducing flavors from four different styles of cheese. The second, and more exciting pairing method, is the "face off." Take two different beer styles like a pilsner and a stout and try them against four to six cheeses. The goal here is to have both beers in front of you and taste them against each cheese. Inevitably, one of the two beers will pair perfectly with each cheese. When tasted in this manner, your senses are blasted with flavors and you need to speak up about what you're tasting. Always take notes; you want to remember what you tasted so that you can bring out the winners next time you have company over.

How do I pick my cheeses? Well, I stick to the classics styles of cheese and always introduce a random cheese that no one would ever think of. In general, you can follow this method when picking cheeses. Pick a fresh goat's milk cheese, like Humboldt Fog, to introduce bright lemon flavors and a clean finish. Then select a soft-ripened cow's milk cheese, like Brie or Explorateur, to bring butter into the discussion. Throw in a pungent, sticky salt-water-washed cheese, like Epoisse or Chimay, to blast your palate with yeast and salt. Finally, choose a blue cheese like Gorgonzola to add flint and spice flavors to the mix.

Some of the perfect pairings I have encountered over the years have been downright sublime. Following are some examples:

Strong cheeses, such as this blue cheese, stand up well to higher alcohol home brews.

Hefeweizen

- Kapuziner Weissbier from Germany with Valençay, a fresh, lemony goat's milk cheese from the Loire Valley in France.
- Ayinger Braü Weisse from Germany with Bleu de Basque a blue cheese with creamy, shortbread biscuit and flint spice flavors.

Lager

- Pilsner Urquell from the Czech Republic with Taleggio, a saltwater-washed cow's milk cheese from Lombardy, Italy.
- Brooklyn Pilsner from New York with Pomerol, a semisoft, buttery cantal (or cheddar) style cheese from Auvergne, France.

Imperial IPA

- Ipswich IPA (Massachusetts) Morbier, a nutty, earthy cow's milk cheese from Jura, France.
- Dogfish 60-Minute IPA from Delaware with Gorgonzola Naturale, a yeasty spicy cow's milk blue cheese from Lombardy, Italy.

Bier de Gardes

- Les Bière Des Sans Culottes from France with Keen's Farmhouse Cheddar, a citrusy, creamy, earthy flavored cow's milk cheese from Somerset, England.
- Portsmouth Biere De Garde from New Hampshire with Pecorino Gran Riserva, a crumbly, savory almond flavored sheep's milk cheese from Tuscany, Italy

Wood-Aged Beer

- Oak-Aged Yeti Imperial Stout from Colorado with Raschera, a semihard clay and yeast-flavored cow's milk cheese from Piedmont, Italy.

Wheat Wine

- Triticus Ale (100 Barrel Series) from Massachusetts with Charollais, an aged goat's milk cheese from Burgundy, France with a dense texture and strong lemon and peanut flavors.

English Ale

- St. Peter's Old-Style Porter from England with Robiola di Serole, a creamy, runny, light lemon and floral flavored goat's milk cheese from Asti, Italy.
- Newcastle Brown Ale from the United Kingdom with Coulommiers, a creamy, butter-straw flavored cow's milk brie from France.

American Stout

- Rogue Chocolate Stout from Oregon with Bayley Hazen Blue, a sweet creamy and flint spice cow's milk blue cheese from Greensboro, Vermont.
- Mocha Java Stout from Massachusetts with Tarentaise, a crumbly, lemony and spicy goat's milk cheese from Savoie, France.

Lambic

- Lindemans Framboise from Belgium with Brebis Ossau, a nutty, dense semi-hard sheep's milk cheese from the Pyrenees with butter and wool flavor finishes.
- Festina Lente from Delaware with Bouq Emissaire, a fresh, dense, lemon and pepper flavored goat's milk cheese from Quebec, Canada.

Beer and Chocolate Pairing

Garrett Oliver, The Brooklyn Brewery

When considering chocolate pairings, most people think first of chocolates and wine. This is a pity, as the wine is unlikely to survive the encounter. Prominent British wine writer Johanna Simon said, "death by chocolate is a common form of wine extermination," and I couldn't agree more. There are a few reasons for this. One is that chocolate's sweetness makes even the most powerful red wines seem overly dry and tough, and they tend to lose their fruit. Also, chocolate is one of the most mouth-coating foods out there; the wine literally tends to "bounce" off the palate. Beer, however, has carbonation, the "scrubbing bubbles," that cleanse the chocolate from your palate. Wine experts will often offer up port, but it fares little better—most ports simply vanish in the presence of chocolate.

Beer works far better with chocolate than any grape-based drink because it can offer flavors with either superior harmony or superior contrast. We're not talking Hershey's or the Whitman's Sampler here, though—you're not going to find what you're looking for in every corner shop. Some of the top names are Valrhona, Scharffen Berger, Leonidas, Teuscher, Jacques Torres, Ghirardelli, Dagoba, Lindt, and for a favorite old standby, Drost. You may well have a local artisan shop in your area making fresh chocolates, and you should definitely have a look there as well; freshness is important when it comes to chocolate.

Taste all of the chocolates at room temperature, somewhere in the 65°F –70°F (18°C–21°C) range, because the fat in chocolate solidifies when chocolate is cold, preventing the flavors from reaching your palate. The beers shouldn't be too cold either;

50°F–55°F (10°C–13°C) will be best, depending on the style. The best glasses for the beer are generally going to be wine glasses, which are shaped to intensify the aromatics of the liquid in the glass. With each pairing, I suggest tasting the beer first, to understand what it tastes like on its own, then taste the chocolate and let it melt well on the tongue and sample the beer with it just before it goes down. Take note of the flavor interactions. Finally, taste more of the beer after the chocolate to see how it works into the aftertaste. Then start smiling!

Tasting Party

First, arrange the chocolates in order of flavor impact. Chocolate is a complicated subject, so I'm going to try and break it down into several bite-sized (sorry) areas: milk chocolate, dark chocolate, filled chocolates, and chocolate truffles.

Let's begin with milk chocolate, which is the most popular type. It consists of 50 percent sugar, 35 percent mild solids, and 15 percent cocoa solids. While its chocolate flavors are less intense than the other types, it melts easily on the tongue and tends to be fairly sweet. Most chocolates can pair well with beers that show a caramel and/or roast character, but with milk chocolate, these flavors can be less concentrated. Among the best pairings for milk chocolate is the strong Scotch ale, tra-

ditionally known as "wee heavy." They are rich, smooth, deeply malty beers with biscuity flavors at the center. Light butterscotch notes are common, as are light coffee and vanilla flavors. They usually check in around 7 to 8 percent alcohol by volume, and the cool Scottish fermentations leave them with considerable residual sweetness. Everything here picks up on the flavors in the milk chocolate; the chocolate can bring out the best in the beer and vice versa. Another possibility here is Bavarian doppelbock, which is a deeply malty beer style of similar strength and flavor.

Many connoisseurs prefer dark chocolate to milk chocolate; it's less sweet, more bitter, and has intense chocolate flavors. It's here that you get into chocolate varietals; chocolates from different countries and regions have distinctly different flavors. Dark chocolate has at least 45 percent cocoa solids and commonly ranges up to 70 percent. Here's where you want to pull out some of the big guns when it comes to roast intensity. Imperial stouts can be brought to bear, showing intense chocolate, coffee and fruit characteristics along with balancing bitterness, roast acidity, and 8 to 12 percent ABV. The fun here is finding the particular relationships between the different beers and chocolates. Many of the chocolates contain some vanilla and spices, which can make the pairings all the more interesting. Avoid overchilling imperial stouts. Stronger beers can be served up to 60°F (16°C) and will show best in red wine glasses or brandy snifters.

Another pairing that can work here is the so-called "double" or "imperial" India pale ale, a type of beer that I've dubbed "San Diego Pale Ale." Whatever you want to call them, they're big, bitter, and brilliantly aromatic. The best of them have real malt character in the center and plenty of fruit to work with. Many chocolates can pair wonderfully with the distinctly orange character of the Simcoe hop variety, or the pineapple aromatics of Horizon. This is a good place to try some of the varietal chocolate samplers that are becoming popular—you can even pair hop varieties to chocolate regions.

Filled chocolates are obviously a bit of a wild card. They can be filled with bittersweet chocolate ganache or any manner of fruit, nuts, or praline preparation. The key to matching here is the filling; the couverture, or coating, is playing a supporting role. For ganache (dark chocolate cream) or nut-based fillings, try imperial stouts, which have the roast intensity to work with either. Dark ganaches are also great with Belgian-style fruit beers, particularly kriek and framboise. It's not hard to see why this works so well. What doesn't tend to work is pairing fruit beers with fruit fillings; the flavors tend to blend strangely, but you can try them for yourself and see. Another favorite filling is coconut, which works very well with imperial stouts, barley wines, and even some of the fruit beers.

For a grand finale, it's hard to beat dark chocolate truffles, the ultimate melt-in-your-mouth chocolate experience. You can even make them yourself. There are hundreds of recipes available online and most take only about an hour to prepare. Truffles are made with heavy cream, butter, and dark chocolate, and the classic type is covered in powdered chocolate as well. Because of all the fresh dairy ingredients, they only keep in the refrigerator for about a week, but don't worry, you'll eat them all before then. They're terrific with imperial stouts and the sweeter versions of Belgian-style fruit beers and abbey ales. They're also great foils for many of the very strong styles being pioneered by American craft brewers, from wood-aged beers to steroidal barley wines.

The important thing, as always with real beer matching, is to be creative by combining flavors to produce something that's more than the sum of its parts. I've tried to fit a big subject into a small space—have fun writing the next chapter yourself!

Breakfast of Champions

Beer is essentially liquid bread and has been nourishing people for centuries. Before modern science recognized that bacteria in drinking water could make the drinker sick, beer was the preferred beverage as the boiling process rendered it more sterile and potable than regular water. Queen Elizabeth I was known to have a pint of strong ale with her breakfast each day.

BEER DINNERS

Hosting a beer dinner needn't be more difficult or complicated than hosting a beer and cheese or a beer and chocolate pairing. The theme of your beer dinner is secondary to the purpose. Your main priority is to slow down, round up a great group of friends and family, and catch up with the people you care about. Once you've got that down, you can get creative with a theme. I've hosted beer dinners centered around such far-flung themes as beat poetry and beer recipes, hip-hop and soul food, and re-creations of ancient meals rediscovered in centuries-old tombs and paired with era/region-appropriate foods.

Recipes Made with Beer

The food recipes in this book are not only designed to be made with beer but to pair perfectly with beer as well. Extreme beer styles are used in these recipes as they will amplify the beer flavors in the dish more apparently than your standard generic lager. Each recipe is sized to satisfy four diners. Great beer should be shared and enjoyed with friends and loved ones so it only makes sense to approach beer dining from the same perspective. This next section provides recipes that can be incorporated into a meal that may or may not have beer in every course you prepare. Whether you are planning a simple, camp-style meal or a fancy white tablecloth dinner, the possibilities that come with cooking with beer are as infinite and exciting as the styles of beer that can be brewed. As with brewing, the use of the best, most natural ingredients will go along way to improving the quality of what you make.

VID-ALE-YA SOUP

This intensely flavorful and hearty soup is easy to prepare and makes a great first course to any beer dinner. The perfect beer style to pair with this soup would be a roasty porter or an inky stout.

PROCESS

1. Clean and cut onions into quarters then slice into ¹/₂-inch (1.3-cm) -thick chunks.

2. Melt butter and olive oil in a cast iron skillet until simmering then add the onion chunks and sauté until translucent. Add garlic and continue to sauté until onions and garlic are soft and beginning to brown.

3. Add the chicken stock and ale, cover the skillet and continue to sauté over medium heat for 20 minutes.

4. Shut off your heat source and stir in the half-and-half and egg yokes.

5. Reheat the soup and portion it into bowls. Top each bowl with Parmesan cheese and crushed black pepper.

6. Serve hot.

INGREDIENTS

2 pounds (900 g) Vidalia onions

2 ounces (55 g) butter

3 cloves garlic

1 tablespoon (30 ml) extra-virgin olive oil

1 pint (475 ml) chicken stock

12 ounces (355 ml) imperial stout or porter

4 ounces (120 ml) half-and-half

4 egg yokes

2 tablespoons (12 g) crushed black pepper

1 ounce (13 g) shaved Parmesan cheese

ALE-SOAKED STEAMERS

The steamers pair well with an American or English brown ale. The English browns tend to be a bit sweeter and the American ones are a bit more hoppy, but both will work well with this dish.

PROCESS

1. Julienne fennel heads and detach rosemary from stems.

2. Combine fennel and rosemary with butter and cook for about 15 minutes, making sure not to burn fennel.

3. Add beer and simmer for an additional 10 minutes.

4. Add steamers and cover until the steamers have opened.

5. Dust with salt and pepper.

6. Ladle clams and sauce into empty soup cans and serve. Be sure to provide good, crusty bread to dip in the leftover sauce.

INGREDIENTS

¹/₂ fennel head

8 sprigs of rosemary

5 ounces (140 g) butter

18 ounces (535 ml) of brown ale

1¹/₂ pounds (700 g) of steamers

1 teaspoon (6 g) pepper

1 tablespoon (18 g) salt

WARM PILSNER CHEVRE SPINACH SALAD

This colorful salad will brighten any festive party and is best paired with a sweeter beer like a Maibock or brown ale. The Demerara sugar you'll need to make the dressing will be available at most homebrew supply sources.

PROCESS

1. Mix the ground cloves, nutmeg, and almond slices and put into a dry sauté pan over medium heat; stir quickly to prevent scorching. Cook until almonds darken noticeably and set aside to cool.

2. Pour honey into the pan and mix in the Demerara sugar over medium heat until it begins to simmer.

3. Add the bottle of pilsner and stir until the dressing begins to simmer.

4. Add the vanilla and olive oil and continue to stir occasionally while simmering for about 5 minutes. As the dressing simmers it will be reduced to approximately half its original volume.

5. Put spinach leaves and dried cranberries in a large salad bowl and top with teaspoon-sized chunks of the chevre. Pour the hot dressing over the salad. The heat will soften the spinach as you toss the salad.

6. Transfer salad to individual bowls and serve warm.

INGREDIENTS

Salad

4 ounces (75 g) dried cranberries

3 cups (60 g) fresh spinach (destemmed and rinsed)

12 ounces (180 g) chevre (goat cheese)

Dressing

1 cup (125 g) almond slices

1/2 teaspoon (2.5 g) ground cloves

1/2 teaspoon (2.5 g) ground nutmeg

5 ounces (210 g) clover honey

6 tablespoons (83 g) demerara sugar

12 ounces (355 ml) pilsner beer (room temperature and flat)

2 teaspoons (10 ml) pure vanilla extract

3 tablespoons (45 ml) extra-virgin olive oil

ZESTY BLUE CHEESE AND IPA DIPPING SAUCE

INGREDIENTS

2 ounces (55 g) butter

5 tablespoons (40 g) flour

6 ounces (175 ml) IPA (room temperature and flat)

2/3 cup (158 ml) half-and-half (room temperature)

1/2 cup (80 g) chopped fresh chives

2 tablespoons (30 g) Dijon mustard

8 ounces (115 g) cream cheese

12 ounces (180 g) crumbled bleu cheese

8 ounces (115 g) shredded cheddar cheese

20 hard breadsticks

The subtle bitterness of the hops in the IPA comes forward in the cooking process and complements the sharp cheese flavors to give the sauce a zesty bite.

PROCESS

1. In a large sauté pan, melt the butter until simmering then add the flour and stir.

2. Add the IPA and half-and-half and stir while simmering for 3 minutes.

3. Add the chopped chives, Dijon mustard, and cream cheese and continue stirring while simmering for 1 minute.

4. As you add the chunks of bleu cheese and cheddar a few ounces (grams) at a time, continue to stir. Wait until each addition of cheese melts into the sauce before making the next addition.

5. After the last cheese addition is fully melted, shut off heat source and transfer sauce into a mixing bowl. Each guest gets five breadsticks for dipping and a pint of hearty, hoppy IPA. Remember, you are among friends, so feel free to double dip.

WITTY CILANTRO MUSSELS

Mussels steamed in beer and served with crusty bread must be the national dish of Belgium. Traditionally, this dish is cooked with just a few flavoring ingredients to allow the goodness of the beer broth to shine through. Serve the mussels in a couple of communal bowls and be sure to include the broth. Half the fun of eating this dish is dipping your bread in the wonderful broth at the base of the bowls. Make sure you have a big empty bowl at the table to discard the shells as you eat. This dish is best enjoyed with a spicy Belgian wit beer, saison, or biere de garde.

PROCESS

Mussels

1. Clean the mussels using cool tap water and a stiff brush. Make sure you discard any mussels that are opened or cracked. Put the clean mussels in a colander and rinse with cool water.

2. Melt the butter in a large soup pot (your stainless brewpot would work well here) over medium heat. Once simmering, add the red onion and celery and cook until everything is well mixed and soft (6 or 7 minutes). Stir occasionally to prevent burning.

3. Add the wit beer to the pot and stir.*

4. Once the mixture is boiling, add your mussels, stir, and cover the pot.

5. After 4 minutes, uncover the pot and sprinkle the fresh cilantro and squeeze in the tangerine juice (discard the peels). Stir the mussels well, pulling up spoonfuls from the broth.

6. Cover and cook for 4 more minutes.

INGREDIENTS

Mussels

5 pounds (2.3 kg) green lipped mussels

3 ounces (83 g) butter

2 big red onions peeled and chopped

3 sticks of celery (chopped into 1/4-inch wide slices)

12 ounces (355 ml) Belgian wit beer

1/2 cup (10 g) fresh cilantro

2 tangerines, halved

Bread

Two loaves crusty French bread

4 ounces (120 ml) extra-virgin olive oil

2 ounces (60 g) finely chopped horseradish

1 ounce (38 g) course salt

7. Open and stir for another minute checking to make sure that all of the mussels have opened.

Bread

*After you've added the beer and are waiting for the mixture to boil, it's a good time to prepare and cook the bread. Cut the loaves in half the long way and lay them out on a baking sheet. Mix the olive oil and horseradish in a bowl and spread it over the bread with a cooking brush. Sprinkle course salt over the top of the bread. Put the bread in your oven at 350°F (177°C, or gas mark 4) until toasted light brown.

8. Put the mussels into two large bowls with the broth evenly distributed in the two bowls. Remove the bread from the oven and serve warm with the mussels.

ULTIMATE STEAK ALE MARINADE

In my family, this recipe is called a "Foush." My father pretends that the name has some meaning in an obscure Italian dialect but I highly doubt it. A Foush is nothing more than a marinade that incorporates vegetables, herbs, and ale sautéed in olive oil. The quality of the meat is as important as the quality of the ingredients for this dish. Treat yourself and friends to a big porterhouse or filet mignon when you are preparing this and pair it with a sweeter robust beer like a bock, a Belgian dubbel, or a barley wine.

INGREDIENTS

- 1/2 cup (120 ml) extra-virgin olive oil
- 1/2 ounce (10 g) chopped shallots
- 1/2 ounce (10 g) chopped garlic
- 1/2 ounce (15 g) crushed juniper berries
- 1 tablespoon (1.7 g) rosemary
- 12 ounces (355 ml) medium body strong beer (Maibock or dubbel)
- 1 tablespoon (6 g) crushed green peppercorns
- 1/2 cup (60 ml) balsamic vinegar
- 4 big, juicy steaks

PROCESS

1. Pour olive oil into large sauté pan over medium heat and allow it to come up to a simmer. Once simmering, add the chopped shallots, chopped garlic, crushed juniper berries, and rosemary needles. Stir and simmer until everything is well mixed and soft.

2. Add the dark beer and continue to simmer over medium heat until volume is reduced by half.

3. Add the Balsamic vinegar and crushed green peppercorns and stir for another minute.

4. Remove sauce from heat. Place steaks in a wide glass bowl and coat them with half of the sauce. Use a fork to poke holes in the steaks as you flip them and cover them with the sauce.

5. Allow the steaks to marinate for at least an hour before cooking them in a hot iron skillet over a bit of olive oil to the desired temperature.

6. Reheat the remaining half of the sauce for a minute over medium heat and spoon it over the finished steaks as they are being served.

SMOKY MAPLE-PORTER BBQ SAUCE

This is the perfect sauce to use when grilling salmon, chicken, or ribs. A sweeter beer will help to cut the heavy, caramely flavors of the fish or meat. I would recommend making this sauce with a porter or stout and serving the finished dish with whichever type of beer you made it with. You can find the dark (or amber) Belgian candi sugar from most homebrew supply sources.

PROCESS

1. Pour olive oil into a cast iron skillet and sauté onions over medium heat until they are soft and translucent. Add garlic and stir occasionally until lightly browned. Set this mixture aside in a bowl.

2. Pour the beer into the cast iron skillet and bring to a simmer over medium heat. Add beef boullion cubes and dark Belgian candi sugar. Stir mixture until all solids are broken down into a solution.

3. Once the mixture reduces by a third in volume, add all other ingredients (including the onion/garlic mixture you set aside) and stir for another minute until the sauce has the consistency of a loose paste.

4. Baste meat with half of the sauce and grill to desired temperature. Reheat the remaining half of the sauce and serve as a condiment with the meal.

INGREDIENTS

1/2 cup (120 ml) extra-virgin olive oil

1 chopped white onion

3 tablespoons (30 g) chopped garlic

12 ounces (355 ml) porter or stout (room temperature and flat)

3 beef boullion cubes

1/2 cup (115 g) dark Belgian candi sugar

1 cup (340 g) pure maple syrup

12 ounces (355 ml) tomato paste

1 tablespoon (15 ml) liquid smoke

2 teaspoons (10 g) crystallized ginger

1 teaspoon (7 g) cumin powder

1 teaspoon (7 g) red chili powder

2 teaspoons (10 g) black pepper

BEER CHEESE SOUP

This soup is best served with a pale ale, IPA, pilsner, or another well-hopped beer.

PROCESS

1. In a large saucepan over low heat, stir together chopped onion, celery, and garlic.

2. Stir in hot pepper sauce, cayenne pepper, salt, and black pepper.

3. Mix in chicken broth and beer and simmer for 15 minutes until veggies are soft. Set aside.

4. In a separate pan, melt butter over low heat, add flour, and cook until golden brown.

5. Slowly stir in milk until thickened.

6. Combine and stir beer mixture into milk and cheese mixture. Add Worcestershire sauce, Dijon mustard, and dry mustard. Bring to simmer and cook for 15 minutes

7. Remove from heat source and ladle into soup bowls.

8. Sprinkle smoked cheddar to cover the top of each soup bowl.

9. Microwave each bowl for 1 minute to melt the cheese.

INGREDIENTS

1/2 cup (40 g) onions

1/2 cup (30 g) celery

2 cloves minced garlic

1 teaspoon (5 ml) hot pepper sauce

1/8 teaspoon (0.6 g) cayenne pepper

1/2 teaspoon (2.5 g) salt

1/2 teaspoon (1.3 g) black pepper

2 cups (475 ml) chicken broth

8 ounces (235 ml) pale ale beer

1/3 cup (75 g) butter

1/3 cup (40 g) flour

4 cups (900 ml) milk or half and half

1 tablespoon (15 g) Dijon mustard

3 teaspoons (15 ml) Worcestershire sauce

2 teaspoons (10 g) dry mustard

1 cup (115 g) shredded smoked cheddar

ST. LOUIS-VIA-EUROPE RIBS

Ribs and other roasted meats pair best with maltier beers as the sweetness of the beer cuts through the spice very effectively. I would recommend serving this with a Belgian dubbel, German Maibock, or even an English barley wine.

PROCESS

1. Using equal parts of each, place all ingredients in large seasoning container and shake until thoroughly mixed. Set mixture aside.

2. Over medium heat reduce beer by half. Remove from heat and stir in BBQ sauce. Set sauce aside.

3. Cover ribs with dry rub and place in shallow baking pan.

4. Add the liquid smoke and fill pan one quarter of the way with water (making sure to not cover ribs).

5. Wrap pan with plastic and foil and bake for 4 hours at 200°F (93°C). Don't go over 250°F (121°C) or you may melt the plastic. Check tenderness, you should be able to pull the meat from the bone easily.

6. Reheat BBQ sauce, slather it on the ribs, and serve.

INGREDIENTS

Dry Rub

1 teaspoon (5 g) kosher salt

1 teaspoon (2 g) paprika

1 teaspoon (2 g) red pepper flake

1 teaspoon (3 g) black pepper

1 teaspoon (3 g) cajun seasoning

1 teaspoon (3 g) granulated garlic

1 teaspoon (2 g) white pepper

1 teaspoon (1 g) oregano

1 teaspoon (3 g) granulated onion

1/2 teaspoon (1.3 ml) liquid smoke

BBQ Sauce

One 32-ounce (945 ml) bottle store-bought BBQ sauce

16 ounces (475 ml) Maibock or Belgian dubbel

4 pounds (1.8 kg) of ribs

TRIPEL-POACHED-PEAR DESSERT

INGREDIENTS

8 ripe pears

10 ounces (285 ml) Belgian tripel (room temperature and flat)

6 teaspoons (40 g) honey or orange liqueur

2 cups (400 g) sugar

2 cinnamon sticks

2 vanilla beans

1/2 cup (10 g) fresh mint leaves

Vanilla ice cream

Golden Belgian ales have a soft, malty sweetness. Since the hop profile on these strong beers is relatively low, they make a great base for dessert reduction sauces. Great on their own, these pears and the syrup are the perfect topping for vanilla bean ice cream. Serve this dessert with a tripel, a fruit lambic, or a tart gueuze.

PROCESS

1. Cut a 2″ x 2″ (5 cm x 5 cm) into the base of each pear to the depth of the core.

2. Boil half a gallon of water in a big pot and submerge the pears in the boiling water for 45 seconds. Remove the pears and discard the boiling water.

3. Dry the pears and let them cool. Peel, and quarter the pears.

4. Pour the tripel, honey (or orange liqueur), sugar, and cinnamon sticks into a big sauté pan. Cut the vanilla bean in half lengthwise and add them to the pan. Stir the mixture over medium heat until all of the sugar is dissolved. Once the syrup hits a boil, reduce heat to a simmer and hold the temperature for 5 minutes or until the liquid volume reduces by half.

5. Carefully place the pear quarters into the hot syrup as it simmers for another 5 minutes or so, occasionally flipping them so they are well soaked in the syrup.

6. Remove the pears from the syrup and place them in a bowl and add the mint leaves to the syrup. Stir and simmer for one more minute. Remove the vanilla beans and cinnamon sticks and discard.

7. Put a couple of scoops of vanilla bean ice cream in four bowls. Portion the pear quarters over the ice cream and drizzle the syrup over each bowl. Serve immediately.

FRUIT BEER ICE CREAM

This recipe works well with any kind of fruit beer, but I like to make it with a tart, pungent Belgian lambic. The idea is to use whatever fruit is in the beer to make the ice cream as well. This recipe is for 2 quarts (2 L) but can easily be halved. You are making an ice cream base and will need an ice cream maker to finish the recipe.

INGREDIENTS

2 cups (475 ml) whole milk

2 cups (475 ml) heavy cream

12 ounces (355 ml) raspberry beer (room temperature and flat)

1/2 cup (115 g) brown sugar

2 cups (220 g) finely chopped raspberries

8 egg yolks

1/2 cup (100 g) sugar

1 teaspoon (5 ml) pure vanilla extract

PROCESS

1. Combine the milk and cream in a large sauté pan and bring the mixture to a boil. Turn off the heat, cover, and let rest for 20 minutes.

2. In a separate medium-size sauté pan, add the fruit beer and brown sugar over medium heat, stirring occasionally, Bring to a boil and immediately shut off the heat source.

3. Whisk the yolks, sugar, and vanilla extract. Next, whisk in a cup of the heated cream mixture and an additional 1/2 cup (120 ml) of cream. Add the rest of the cream in as you whisk vigorously. Once this is all well mixed, add it back to your empty large sauté pan. Cook the mixture over medium heat, stirring occasionally with a large wooden spoon until it is thick enough to stick to the spoon. This should take about 10 minutes. Remove from heat source.

4. Use a tight mesh strainer to pour the mixture into a large bowl and shake in the small chunks of raspberries.

5. Place the bowl in your refrigerator overnight, then run it through your ice cream maker following the directions as you would for your particular machine.

6. Parcel out the ice cream to dinner guests, serve accompanied with a fruit beer, and enjoy.

COWBOY SUNDAY DESSERT

You'll want a roasty dark to enhance the chocolate flavor. I would recommend an Irish stout, porter, or an imperial stout. A pale-ale reduction is a tasy touch.

INGREDIENTS

18 ounces (535 ml) stout

6 ounces (175 ml) chocolate syrup

Vanilla ice cream

Whipped cream

9 ounces (268 ml) pale ale

1/2 cup (115 g) brown sugar

PROCESS

1. Over medium heat, reduce stout volume by half.

2. Stir in chocolate syrup and continue to reduce until thick.

3. Over medium heat, reduce ale volume by half.

4. Stir in brown sugar and continue to reduce until thick.

5. Drizzle hot chocolate syrup over bowls of ice cream and serve.

6. Top with whipped cream and a splash of pale ale reduction and serve.

CONCLUSION

Now that you've made your first batches of homebrew and have the recipes and inspiration to create memorable dinners and tastings, it's time to savor the fruits of your labor and share your new hobby with your friends and family. As both a homebrewer and a commercial brewer, I can assure you that there is nothing more rewarding than seeing someone whose company you enjoy and whose opinion you value, fall in love with a beer you've created. Breaking bread, clinking pints, and just plain talking with the people we care for should be the raison d'être in each of our lives. Of course, you'll probably want to do more than just drink your carefully crafted brews. After all the time and effort you've put into this endeavor, a little presentation is certainly warranted. This is the perfect opportunity to tell your friends about the beers you've made and explain some of what you've learned. Don't just share your beer; share your knowledge.

Appendix: Hop Varieties

Amarillo is an aroma-type cultivar of recent origin, discovered and introduced by Virgil Gamache Farms Inc. Used for its aromatic properties and also for its bittering properties due to its lower cohumulone content. Earthy musk with strong citrus notes.

Cascade is an aroma-type cultivar that originated as the first commercial hop from the USDA-ARS breeding program. Used for its aromatic properties hints of grapefruit, floral and pine.

Centennial is an aroma-type cultivar that is used for its aromatic properties and bittering potential. Well-balanced citrus and floral notes.

Chinook is a bittering variety with aroma characteristics released in May 1985. It was bred by crossing a Petham Golding with the USDA 63012 male. Used for its high proportion of bittering from alpha-acids plus its aromatic characteristics. Strong notes of grapefruit, spice, and pine.

Clusters originated from mass selection of the cluster hop, which is an old American cultivar. It is suggested that they arose from hybridization of varieties, imported by Dutch and English settlers and indigenous male hops. Used as a kettle hop for bittering, floral and spicy.

Czech Saaz aroma land-race variety selected in the area of the same name. A noble hop that is spicy with hints of citrus.

Fuggles is an aroma-type cultivar selected in England as a chance seedling in 1861. It reached its peak in the UK in 1949 when 78 percent of the English crops were grown as Fuggles. Used for its aromatic properties.

Goldings and East Kent Golding are part of a group of aroma-type cultivars originating in England. Over the decades, the group has been changed and widened. Mostly named after villages in East Kent, (Petham, Rothersham, Canterbury, Eastwell) or hop farmers who grew them (Amos's Early Bird, Cobbs). English Goldings grown in East Kent, are a premium hop, called East Kent Golding and should not be confused with U.K. Goldings, which are grown in other areas. The cultivar grown in the U.S. (Oregon and Washington State) is a Canterbury Golding. Used for its gentle aromatic properties and crisp finish.

Hallertau is an aroma-type cultivar that originated in Germany as a land-race hop. Used for its mild yet spicy aromatic properties.

Magnum is a bittering/aroma type cultivar, bred in 1980 at Huell, the German Hop Research Institute. Used for its bittering value and quality.

Northern Brewer is a bittering-type cultivar, bred in 1934 in England. Northern Brewer has been used in the breeding process of many newer varieties. Grown in England, Belgium, Germany and the U.S. Northern Brewer has pronounced aroma compared to the typical bittering hop, sometimes grassy.

Perle is an aroma-type cultivar, bred in 1978 in Germany from Northern Brewer. It is grown in Germany, Belgium and the U.S. Used for both its bittering quality and floral aroma.

Simcoe is a bittering/aroma type cultivar bred by Yakima Chief Ranches. Used for its aromatic and especially for its bittering properties due to its low cohumulone content properties. Complex aroma; strong, assertive, earthy musk.

Sterling is an aroma cultivar. Used for its aromatic properties, similar to Saaz. Very mild, spicy, and earthy.

Styrian Golding Derivative of Fuggles, grown in Slovenia. Widespread acceptance, very soft yet spicy.

Tettnanger is an aroma-type cultivar that originated in the Tettnang hop-growing area of Germany as a land-race hop. It is grown in the U.S.A. in Oregon and Washington state. Used for its somewhat spicy aromatic properties.

Tomahawk is a bittering hop of recent origin, bred by Charles Zimmermann. It is the first commercially grown Super Alpha variety. Strong, aggressive pungency.

Warrior is a bittering hop of a recent origin, bred by Yakima Chief Ranches. Low cohumulone content delivers clean finish with forward palate bitterness.

Willamette is a triploid aroma-type hop, that originated in the mid 1970's and is a seedling of Fuggle. It is a very popular aroma hop, contributing in 1998 to 18 percent of the total hop crop in the U.S. Use for its aromatic properties and moderate bittering.

Vanguard is a diploid seedling developed in 1982. It was released for cultivation in 1997. Used for its aromatic properties and low cohumulone similar to the Hallertau cultivar. Can have wonderful black current notes.

Glossary of Common Brewing Terms

Aerate The process of dissolving air into wort at the beginning of fermentation to promote yeast cell growth.

Ale yeast A top fermenting yeast that ferments best at warmer temperatures. This yeast is anaerobic and will settle to the bottom of the carboy after fermentation.

Alpha acids The amount of bitterness in hops. Low alpha hops are in the 2 to 5 percent range; high alpha hops are in the 9 percent and over range. Brewers also calibrate hopping volumes in IBUs (International Bittering Units) that tell how bitter the beer is, whereas alpha acids indicate how bitter the hops themselves are.

Airlock The device used to allow gas to escape but prevent air from entering the neck of the carboy of fermenting beer.

Attenuation The reduction of sugars as a result of the fermentation process.

Barley The grain that provides the most common source of fermentable sugar in beer.

Beta acid A chemical found in the lupulin gland of hops.

Brewpot The pot, preferably stainless steel, that you brew your beer in.

Carboy The preferred fermenting and aging vessel used in homebrewing. Usually this glass container is either 5 or 6.5 gallons (19 L or 25 L) and has a thin neck at the top into which you can insert a rubber stopper and fermentation lock.

Demerara sugar A brown sugar that is commonly used in brewing.

Dry hopping The addition of whole leaf or palletized hops during or after primary fermentation.

Ester A fermentation byproduct that contributes fruity characteristics to the aroma and flavor of the beer.

Fermentation The natural process by which yeast converts sugar to alcohol and the byproduct in carbon dioxide.

Fermenter The vessel to which you add the wort and yeast to ferment into beer.

Fermentation lock The plastic device that fits into the top of your fermenting bucket or carboy. It allows carbon dioxide to escape but prevents unsterile air from getting into your beer.

Finish hops Also called aroma hops, Pelletized or whole-leaf hops used toward the end of the boil. The late addition of these hops will contribute more hop aroma in the smell of the beer than hop flavor in the taste.

Fining A clarifying procedure used in the brewing process. Usually these gelatinous products (isinglass and Irish moss are most common) are added to brighten and clarify the beer.

Gravity This term is used three ways in homebrewing—specific, original, and final. Specific gravity is the measure of the density of beer compared to the density of water. If a reading is higher than 1.000 than the liquid is more dense than water. The higher the concentrations of sugar in a beer the higher the gravity. Original gravity is the density of the beer before it starts to ferment. Final gravity is the density of the beer after it has finished fermenting.

Hydrometer A glass, calibrated, measuring device that reveals the specific gravity of a liquid.

Hot break The settling of protein and hop solids, that condense and collect in the bottom of your kettle after the beer has been boiled.

Hops A perennial flowering vine; the female buds are used in flavoring, bittering, and preserving beer.

Hop pellets Hop buds that have been processed and compressed.

Hop tea A solution of hops and hot water.

Kiln The equipment used to reduce moisture during the malt and hop manufacturing processes.

Krausen The fluffy foam that grows on the top of your wort as it begins to ferment.

Lager yeast A family of brewing yeasts that work best at cooler temperatures and is considered a bottom-fermenting yeast because it doesn't form a head and ferments within, and not on top of the beer.

Lager (verb) Derived from the German term for storage, it means to age or condition the beer for extended periods of time at cool temperatures.

Lambic Belgian style beers fermented via wild yeast and bacteria present in the air and aged in wood barrels.

Lovibond A measurement scale that calibrates the level of color in barley.

Malt Any cereal grain that has gone through the malting process.

Malted barley This is the form that brewers use barley in—it has been partially germinated then quickly dried so that sugars, starches, and enzymes can be accessed through the brewing process.

Malt extract Could be called wort concentrate—A syrup or powder that has been created by condensing wort or prefermented beer. The most common form of barley sugars in novice home-brewing.

Maltose Malt sugar

Maltster A person who works in a malting facility.

Mash Mixing malt and hot water to convert starches into sugars.

Mashing Hydrating the milled malted barley to convert the grain starches into sugars. The process of conversion occurs between 140°F and 160°F (60°C and 70°C) as with the specialty grain cheesecloth methods featured in the recipes in this book.

Mash tun The vessel in which you mash.

Pitching The adding of yeast to the wort after it has come down to a desired temperature. The pitching rate of a beer is determined by calculating how many yeast cells are required to ferment a certain volume of beer.

Priming The method by which you prepare your beer to carbonate by adding sugar to the beer just before transferring it into the bottles.

Racking The term for transferring wort or beer from one vessel to another. A siphon and hose are commonly used in racking beer that has finished fermenting so as to leave the unwanted yeast solids behind.

Saccharomyces cerevisiae The Latin name for any ale or lager yeast.

Sanitize The process of cleaning and sterilizing any surface that comes into contact with your beer or your brewing materials. Yeast is highly susceptible to mutation and poor fermentation in a poorly sanitized environment.

Sparging The process of rinsing the grains with hot water to optimize the collection of sugars.

Steep Adding grains or hops to hot but not boiling wort.

Whole-leaf hops Hops leafs that have been dried but not compressed into pellets and are ready to be used in their natural state.

Wort The term used for beer (or barley-water) before fermentation has commenced.

Yeast The living organism that coverts sugar into alcohol. In addition to driving the fermentation process, certain yeast strains will contribute different flavors and aromas to different beers. The fermentation process is anaerobic and, at a certain concentration, alcohol becomes toxic to the yeast and breaks down its cell wall. That is why no naturally fermented beer can be as strong as a distilled spirit…although we'll keep trying.

Resources

Books

Altbier
History, Brewing Techniques, Recipes
By Horst D. Dornbusch
Brewers Publications, 1998

Analysis of Brewing Techniques, An
By George Fix and Laurie Fix
Brewers Publications, 1997

Barley Wine
History, Brewing Techniques, Recipes
By Fal Allen and Dick Cantwell
Brewers Publications, 1998

Bavarian Helles
History, Brewing Techniques, Recipes
By Horst D. Dornbusch
Brewers Publications, 2000

Belgian Ale
By Pierre Rajotte
Brewers Publications, 1992

Bock
By Darryl Richman
Brewers Publications, 1994

Brew Like a Monk
By Stan Herronomous

Continental Pilsner
By David Miller
Brewers Publications, 1990

Designing Great Beers
The Ultimate Guide to Brewing Classic Beer Styles
By Ray Daniels
Brewers Publications, 1996

Dictionary of Beer and Brewing
Second Edition
Compiled by Dan Rabin
and Carl Forget
Brewers Publications, 1997

Essentials of Beer Style, The
A Catalog of Classic Beer Styles for Brewers and Beer Enthusiasts
By Fred Eckhardt
Fred Eckhardt Associates Inc.

Farmhouse Ales
Culture and Craftsmanship in the Belgian Tradition
By Phil Markowski
Brewers Publications, 2004

German Wheat Beer
By Eric Warner
Brewers Publications, 1992

Complete Joy of Homebrewing
Everything You Need to Get Started in Homebrewing
By Charlie Papazian
Collins; 3rd edition, 2003

Kölsch
History, Brewing Techniques, Recipes
By Eric Warner
Brewers Publications, 1998

Michael Jackson's Great Beer Guide
The World's 500 Beer Classics
By Michael Jackson and Sharon Lucas

Michael Jackson's World Beer Hunter
By Michael Jackson
The World's Top Breweries
—CD-rom included

Michael Jackson's Great Beers of Belgium
Brewing Styles from the Beer Capitol of the World
By Michael Jackson

Mild Ale
History, Brewing Techniques, Recipes
By David Sutula
Brewers Publications, 1999

New Brewing Lager Beer
The Most Comprehensive Book for Home- and Microbrewers
By Gregory J. Noonan
Brewers Publications, 1996

Oktoberfest, Vienna, Märzen
By George Fix and Laurie Fix
Brewers Publications, 1992

Pale Ale
History, Brewing Techniques, Recipes
Second Edition
By Terry Foster, Ph.D.
Brewers Publications, 1999

Porter
By Terry Foster, Ph.D.
Brewers Publications, 1992

Principles of Brewing Science
Second Edition
By George Fix, Ph.D.
Brewers Publications, 1999

Radical Brewing
By Randy Mosher
Brewers Publications, 2004

Sacred and Herbal Healing Beers
The Secrets of Ancient Fermentation
By Stephen Harrod Buhner
Brewers Publications, 1998

Scotch Ale
By Gregory J. Noonan
Brewers Publications, 1993

Smoked Beers
History, Brewing Techniques, Recipes
By Ray Daniels and Geoff Larson
Brewers Publications, 2000

Stout
By Michael J. Lewis, Ph.D.
Brewers Publications, 1996

Ultimate Beer
The Ultimate Guide to Classic Brewing
By Michael Jackson

Wild Brews
Beer Beyond the Influence of Brewer's Yeast
By Jeff Sparrow
Brewers Publications, 2005

Magazines and Journals

Zymurgy: Journal of the American Homebrewers Association
www.homebrewersassociation.org

Ale Street News
www.alestreetnews.com

All About Beer
www.allaboutbeer.com

American Brewer
www.ambrew.com

BYO
www.byo.com

Brewing Techniques
www.brewingtechniques.com

Celebrator
www.celebrator.com

Mid-Atlantic Brewing
www.brewingnews.com/mid-atlantic/

Yankee Brew News
www.brewingnews.com/yankeebrew/

Homebrew Supplies

Annapolis Homebrew Shop
www.annapolishomebrew.com

Beer, Beer, and More Beer
www.morebeer.com

Hop Tech
www.hoptech.com

Maryland Homebrew
www.mdhb.com

Party Pig
www.partypig.com

Xtreme Brewing Company
www.xtremebrewing.com
Provides prepackaged ingredients to make any of the recipes in this book.

Websites

American Homebrewers Association (AHA)
www.homebrewersassociation.org
Official site of the AHA and
Zymurgy: Journal of the AHA

Beer Advocate
www.beeradvocate.com
An in-depth, hardcore beer enthusiast's website

Beer Cook
www.beercook.com
All about cooking with beer and pairing beer with food

Brewer's Association Beertown
www.craftbeer.com
Home of the Brewers Association. The largest online community of professional and home brewers

Canadian Real Beer
www.realbeer.com/canada
The Canadian beer index for all things beer in the great white north

New Zealand Brewers' Network
www.brewing.co.nz
For all things beer in New Zealand and Downunder

Real Beer
www.realbeer.com
An insightful site for the beer enthusiast

Ratebeer
www.ratebeer.com
A resource for all sorts of beer-related information

Yeast

For additional information on specific yeast strains found in this book, reference the websites for White Labs and Wyeast Laboratories.

White Labs
564 Trade Street
San Diego, CA USA 92121
Tel: 858.693.3441
Fax: 858.693.1026
www.whitelabs.com

Wyeast Laboratories, Inc
PO Box 146
Odell, OR USA 97044
Tel: 541.354.1335
Fax: 541.354.3449
www.wyeastlab.com

E-Brew and Brewing Software

Promash
Download software to create three recipes without purchase.
www.promash.com

Beer Info
www.beerinfo.com/vlib/software.html

Beer Tools
www.beertools.com

Beer Smith
www.beersmith.com

Index

ACKNOWLEDGMENTS

I'd like to begin with a big wet kiss for my wife, Mariah, whose patience and support throughout this project has been critical. Next, I'd like to thank my amazing children, Sam and Grier, who make me as excited to get home at night as I am to get to the brewery in the morning. I owe a huge debt of gratitude to Doug Griffith, who worked very hard on this book with me, who knows and loves brewing as much as I do, and has been there for Dogfish Head every step of the way. I'd like to thank all of the writers, beer folk, and brewers who helped me so much with this book including Robert Aguilera, Garrett Oliver, Adam Avery, Vinnie Cilerzo, Tomme Arthur, Rob Tod, George Hummel, Dave Logsdon, Bryan Selders, Mike Gerhart, Randy Mosher, Dave White, and Jim Boyd. Thanks to our amazing photographer, Kevin Fleming, and stylist Fred Mazzeo for all of their help making this book look so good. Last, but certainly foremost in making this book come together so well, I'd like to thank my editor, Candice Janco, and copy editor, Maia Merrill.

ABOUT THE AUTHOR

When **Sam Calagione** opened Dogfish Head Craft Brewery in 1995 it was the smallest commercial brewery in America, making 10 gallons of beer at a time. Today, Dogfish Head is among the fastest growing breweries in the country. Dogfish Head has focused on brewing stronger, more exotic beers since the day it opened as its motto, "off-centered ales for off-centered people," attests to. Dogfish Head has grown into a 90-person company with a restaurant, brewery, and distillery in Rehoboth Beach, an alehouse in Maryland, and a production brewery in Milton, Delaware. Dogfish sells beer in 27 states and 3 countries. Dogfish Head was the only brewery in America (out of 1,400) to be named to the *Inc.* 500 list of the fastest-growing private companies in the country for 2004 and 2005. Sam is also the author of *Brewing up a Business* and the forthcoming book, *He Said Beer, She Said Wine*. He lives in Lewes, Delaware, with his wife Mariah and children, Sam and Grier.